Safe Sanctuaries for Youth

Reducing the Risk of Abuse in Youth Ministries

by Joy Thornburg Melton

DISCIPLESHIP RESOURCES

PO BOX 340003 • NASHVILLE, TN 37203-0003
www.discipleshipresources.org

Dedication

This book is dedicated, with gratitude, to Susan Hay, Terry Carty, and Mike Selleck, who have demonstrated a measure of compassion and integrity in youth ministry that has inspired a community of young Christians.

It is also dedicated to Jennifer Bowden for the nurturing love she has delivered to the community of young Christians in Atlanta, Georgia.

Finally, this work is dedicated to David and Kathryn Melton, who guide me every day.

Reprinted 2004

Cover and book design by Joey McNair

Edited by Linda R. Whited and Heidi L. Hewitt

Library of Congress Card Catalog No. 2002117848

ISBN 0-88177-404-9

This resource is published by Discipleship Resources in the hope that it will help congregations in planning. Discipleship Resources and the General Board of Discipleship are not engaged in legal, accounting, or other professional advising services. If legal advice or other expert assistance is required, the services of a professional advisor should be sought. This book does not establish a standard of care for local churches. Each local church makes its own decisions and determines what is best for it, and this book is intended only to provide information that may be helpful to some churches.

DR404

Contents

Our Mandate

AS CHRISTIANS, we live according to the gospel of Jesus Christ. Our Christian heritage derives from that of the ancient Hebrews. We accept the tradition and experience set forth in the Old Testament, or Hebrew Scriptures, as our own. In the history of the ancient Hebrews, we find a deeply rooted legacy of justice and mercy centered in the community of faith (Leviticus 19:15; Deuteronomy 24:17; Isaiah 1:17; Isaiah 56:1; Amos 5:24; Micah 6:8). We also find a strong tradition of hospitality and generosity demonstrated by the people of faith (Leviticus 19:10 and Isaiah 58:10-12).

Justice and hospitality were essential elements of the covenant between the people and God. Worship was the lifeblood of that covenant. Throughout the history of the Hebrew people, their practice of worshiping God in holy places is recorded. Sometimes the holy place of worship was no more than a small tent or a pile of rocks on the plains. At other times, the place for worship was a beautifully ornate temple with many grand chambers. No matter what the place of worship looked like, the people treasured it as a holy place, a sanctuary where they were able to worship in safety and harmony (Psalm 20:1-2 and 27:4-5). Today, we must remember that our churches are holy places of sanctuary for the children of God. Perhaps now, more than ever, we must do all we can to maintain our churches as nurturing, sheltering places for our youth. Teenagers in our faith communities face fears and stresses that many of us, as parents, never imagined would be possible. As this book was being written, the news media was focused on a series of murders and attempted murders that included the critical injury of a middle school student by an unidentified sniper as the student walked into his school. Schools in the area were locked down and outdoor activities, even homecoming festivities, were cancelled. Counselors were provided at area schools to help students face and cope with the fears that naturally follow such an event. Churches mobilized their resources to provide counseling, encouragement, and opportunities for prayer and fellowship. Our churches must continue to be places where people of all ages can come together for worship, study, and service, with the assurance that they are safe and secure in the community of faith.

The New Testament makes clear that, as Christians, we continue in a covenant relationship with God and with the whole community of faith. In Luke 2:21-23, Mary and Joseph present Jesus for dedication to God, according to their tradition. That tradition continues today in our communities of faith whenever we present our children and youth for baptism. Later, the Gospel of Luke records another visit of Mary, Joseph, and Jesus to their center of worship, Jerusalem (2:41-52). Jesus, who was a youth by then, felt at home, secure, and comfortable there. The faith community, or congregation, in which he had been raised had included him since his childhood, so he felt as if he belonged there.

The model set forth in the story of Jesus' family is the model we want for our families and congregations today. We must live just and generous lives, following the commandments set forth by Jesus Christ. Jesus plainly taught that children and youth are to be included and provided for within the community of faith (Matthew 18:5-6 and Luke 18:15-17). Throughout the history of the Christian church, children and youth have been included in the worship and ministry of the faith community. Today, the church may be the only place where some teenagers find the unconditional love and care they so desperately need to grow, to thrive, and to become faithful people. As Christians, we must take our responsibilities to our youth seriously, always attending to their spiritual growth and nurturing. We fail in our responsibilities if we neglect to take adequate precautions against physical and emotional abuse in our churches. It is unlikely that we can completely prevent such abuse in every circumstance. Yet, it is possible for us to greatly reduce the risk by following a thorough and practical policy of prevention.

Sexual abuse of youth is a tragic reality in our communities. Although we would much prefer to deny it, sexual abuse of youth in our churches is an inescapable fact. Nearly every day this year, we have heard reports in the media about abuse perpetrated in a church or at a church-sponsored program. When I began work in the ministry more than two decades ago, there was little public awareness of the existence of sexual abuse in the church. Now, it is the single most traumatic issue I deal with in my work as an attorney and a United Methodist minister. Youth ministers and other workers with youth are often the people most trusted by youth. When those adults take advantage of that trust and abuse teens, the physical and emotional injuries are devastating. For example, imagine the traumatic suffering within a youth group when it is learned that the youth minister has been repeatedly sexually abusing two of the senior-high girls

TODAY, THE CHURCH MAY BE the only place where some teenagers find the unconditional love and care they so desperately need to grow, to thrive, and to become faithful people.

in the group. Imagine the horror within a church when it is discovered that the director of the youth sports program has been sexually abusing members of the athletic teams under his supervision. These are just two examples of the many cases that have been in the news recently. The churches, the teens, and the teens' families will, no doubt, continue to suffer for years to come.

United Methodist churches have historically worked to assure that children and teens in the communities were cared for with food, clothing, education, and an affirmation of value and self-worth. In many communities, The United Methodist Church (through its predecessor denominations) was the first to provide kindergarten for the children of the community, daycare centers for children of working parents, and Sunday schools where the children heard about God's love and presence in daily life. Many United Methodist churches have been leaders in providing afterschool athletics and tutoring for youth. Today, these traditions continue and provide a solid foundation from which we can address the need for prevention of all forms of abuse of our youth.

When allegations of abuse of youth and children in the church are made, whether they eventually are proven true or false, everyone in the church suffers. The youth victim and his or her family suffer encompassing pain. The congregation suffers the trauma of knowing that its life-giving covenant has been broken. The family of the perpetrator suffers intense humiliation and a likely breakup of the family unit. Often when such allegations are made, litigation is the result. Criminal charges may be brought against the suspected perpetrator, and a civil lawsuit may be filed to recover monetary damages from the accused and from the local church. The costs of litigation, regardless of the outcome, are astronomical—financially, emotionally, and spiritually. These losses are experienced by all who are involved. In many such situations, it takes years to feel that the wholeness of the community of faith has been restored.

Even when allegations of sexual abuse of a youth or a child are proven false, the grief and trauma experienced within the church take an enormous toll. The person who is falsely accused and his or her family are terribly wronged and humiliated. The congregation is guilt-ridden about how abuse could happen in their midst; then the congregation suffers with the accused when the allegations are proven false. Finally, the victim who made false allegations needs the love and nurture of the faith community.

Notes:

AS CHRISTIANS, WE MUST
take our responsibilities to our youth seriously, always attending to their spiritual growth and nurturing.

Notes:

The 1996 General Conference of The United Methodist Church adopted a resolution aimed at reducing the risk of child sexual abuse in the church. The substance of this resolution encompasses the protection of children and youth all the way through high school age. The full text of this resolution is printed on pages 8–10. As you read it, you will notice that specific steps are to be taken by local churches, annual conferences, the General Board of Discipleship, and the General Board of Global Ministries. This book has been created to assist your conference or local church as you work through these steps.

Abuse prevention and risk-reduction policies and procedures are essential for every congregation, not only for the protection and safety of our youth and children (all those under the age of eighteen) but also for our volunteer and paid workers with children and youth. Local congregations differ in the ways they engage in ministry with youth. Therefore, each congregation's need for prevention policies and guidelines will be somewhat different from the others.

The gospel calls us to be engaged in ministry with youth. We must not allow the risks to undermine or stop our ministry. Rather, we must

- acknowledge the risks and develop a practical plan to reduce them;
- take steps to prevent harm to our youth and workers with youth;
- continue to answer the gospel's imperative to be in ministry with youth, making a difference in their lives.

ABUSE PREVENTION AND
risk-reduction policies and procedures are essential for every congregation.

This book is offered as a source of guidance and of appropriate model policies for your congregation as it creates a substantive plan of abuse prevention. *Safe Sanctuaries for Youth* can be a valuable resource for your congregation or annual conference as it undertakes to make the gospel's mandate real by providing a safe and wholly secure place in which youth may experience the abiding love of God and fellowship in the community of faith.

Reducing the Risk of Child Sexual Abuse in the Church*

Jesus said, "Whoever welcomes [a] child ... welcomes me" (Matthew 18:5). Children are our present and our future, our hope, our teachers, our inspiration. They are full participants in the life of the church and in the realm of God.

Jesus also said, "If any of you put a stumbling block before one of these little ones ... it would be better for you if a great millstone were fastened around your neck and you were drowned in the depth of the sea" (Matthew 18:6). Our Christian faith calls us to offer both hospitality and protection to the little ones, the children. The Social Principles of The United Methodist Church state that "children must be protected from economic, physical, emotional, and sexual exploitation and abuse" (¶ 162C).

Tragically, churches have not always been safe places for children. Child sexual abuse, exploitation, and ritual abuse** occur in churches, both large and small, urban and rural. The problem cuts across all economic, cultural, and racial lines. It is real, and it appears to be increasing. Most annual conferences can cite specific incidents of child sexual abuse and exploitation within churches. Virtually every congregation has among its members adult survivors of early sexual trauma.

Such incidents are devastating to all who are involved: the child, the family, the local church, and its leaders. Increasingly, churches are torn apart by the legal, emotional, and monetary consequences of litigation following allegations of abuse.

God calls us to make our churches safe places, protecting children and other vulnerable persons from sexual and ritual abuse. God calls us to create communities of faith where children and adults grow safe and strong. In response to this churchwide challenge, the following steps should be taken to reduce the risk of child sexual abuse:

A. *Local churches* should:
1. develop and implement an ongoing education plan for the congregation and its leaders on the reality of child abuse, risk factors leading to child abuse, and strategies for prevention;
2. adopt screening procedures (use of application forms, interviews, reference checks, background clearance, and so forth) for workers (paid and unpaid) directly or indirectly involved in the care of children and youth;
3. develop and implement safety procedures for church activities such as having two or more nonrelated adults present in classroom or activity; leaving doors open and installing half-doors or windows in doors or halls; providing hall monitors; instituting sign-in and sign-out procedures for children ages ten or younger; and so forth;
4. advise children and young persons of an agency or a person outside as well as within the local church whom they can contact for advice and help if they have suffered abuse;
5. carry liability insurance that includes sexual abuse coverage;

THE GENERAL CONFERENCE OF The United Methodist Church adopted this resolution aimed at reducing the risk of child sexual abuse in the church.

Notes:

6. assist the development of awareness and self-protection skills for children and youth through special curriculum and activities; and
7. be familiar with annual conference and other church policies regarding clergy sexual misconduct.

B. *Annual conferences* should:
1. develop safety and risk-reducing policies and procedures for conference-sponsored events such as camps, retreats, youth gatherings, childcare at conference events, mission trips, and so forth; and
2. develop guidelines and training processes for use by church leaders who carry responsibility for prevention of child abuse in local churches. Both sets of policies shall be developed by a task force appointed by the cabinet in cooperation with appropriate conference agencies. These policies shall be approved by the annual conference and assigned to a conference agency for implementation. It is suggested that the policies be circulated in conference publications and shared with lay professionals and clergy at district or conference seminars.

C. *The General Board of Discipleship and the General Board of Global Ministries* should cooperatively develop and/or identify and promote the following resources:

1. sample policies, procedures, forms, and so forth for reducing the risk of sexual abuse and exploitation of children and youth in local churches, both in relation to their own sponsored programs and to any outreach ministries or other programs for children or youth that use church space;
2. child abuse prevention curriculum for use in local churches;
3. training opportunities and other educational resources on child sexual abuse and exploitation and on ritual abuse; and
4. resources on healing for those who have experienced childhood sexual trauma.

* This is Resolution 59 in *The Book of Resolutions of The United Methodist Church—2004*. Copyright © 2004 by The United Methodist Publishing House. Used by permission.

** "Ritual abuse" refers to abusive acts committed as part of ceremonies or rites; ritual abusers are often related to cults, or pretend to be.

See ¶ 162C in *The Book of Discipline of The United Methodist Church—2004*.

The Scope
of the Problem

EVERY SUNDAY our local congregations gather for worship, and many of them conduct the service of baptism for youth, children, or adults. In the congregation where I worship, we have two worship services each Sunday. Almost every week both our services include baptisms. At least once a year our congregation celebrates confirmation for the youth who have completed their confirmation studies and have decided to profess their Christian faith. This year our confirmation class includes nearly seventy youth. Confirmation day will be a day of unforgettable celebration for these youth and their families, as well as for our whole congregation. Every congregation celebrates confirmation, whether there is one or one hundred young Christians to be confirmed, for in this way, we recognize anew the presence and power of God in a new generation of believers.

At the worship service in which the youth are confirmed, our pastor will address the entire congregation, saying, "Brothers and sisters, I commend to your love and care these persons whom we this day receive into the [professing] membership of this congregation. Do all in your power to increase their faith, confirm their hope, and perfect them in love." The congregation will respond with the following promise and covenant, "We rejoice to recognize you as [professing] members of Christ's holy church, and bid you welcome to this congregation of The United Methodist Church. With you we renew our vows to uphold it by our prayers, our presence, our gifts, and our service. With God's help we will so order our lives after the example of Christ that, surrounded by steadfast love, you may be established in the faith, and confirmed and strengthened in the way that leads to life eternal" ("Baptismal Covenant III," *The United Methodist Hymnal;* pages 48–49). Making this promise gives each and every person in the congregation a sacred role and responsibility in the lives of the newly confirmed youth.

How often have you stopped to think about what your sacred responsibility is for the youth in your congregation? How can your congregation flesh out that responsibility? All the members of our congregations understand that at the baptism or confirmation of youth and children we are not simply spectators but

Notes:

WHY IMPLEMENT A PLAN
to prevent abuse? Because our church is a community of faith, a safe haven and sanctuary where youth can be confirmed and strengthened in the way that leads to life eternal.

are true participants. By our pledge, we are committed to lead our lives in ways that demonstrate to the youth the ways of Christ and the highest standards of Christian discipleship. Therefore, we are called to assure that our churches are places where youth can experience fellowship and nurture without fear of being injured or abused. Unfortunately, we cannot accomplish our goal by simply throwing open the doors of the church building and proclaiming, "Let's have some fellowship!" Today, we must live out our responsibility by organizing our ministries with youth in ways that will protect them as they explore what for them are the new and abstract mysteries of Christian faith. Furthermore, we must organize our ministries in ways that will protect the adults who work with youth from unfounded and false allegations of abuse or inappropriate behavior. Without a strong cadre of adult leaders who feel trusted and valued by the church, youth ministry will come to a screeching halt.

Research has shown convincingly that an overwhelming majority of American teenagers believe in God. A 1992 poll conducted by Gallup found that ninety-five percent of teenagers believe in God, forty-two percent pray alone frequently, thirty-six percent read Scriptures at least weekly, and forty-five percent belong to a church-sponsored youth group and attend worship services weekly. The same research indicates that youth practicing their faith are individuals who possess a greater measure of prosocial values and demonstrate more caring behaviors than age-group peers who lack involvement with religious groups. Approximately seventy-five percent of teens are members of religious groups. Within these groups, sixty-two percent of the members do volunteer service work and fifty-six percent make charitable contributions. These facts are mirrored in the findings of other research that show that church attendance and religious affiliation are positively associated with concern for the needy and willingness to help others. When we pay attention to findings such as these, we realize that the data substantiates what we intuitively know and feel about the importance of providing opportunities for our youth to actively participate in the community of faith. Opportunities for participation in youth ministry provide formative experiences that support teens as they explore and acquire values consistent with our Christian faith.

Another dimension needs to be considered: The teenager's affiliation with a community of faith is a source of strength to him or her for reducing high-risk behaviors, such as alcohol and drug use, antisocial behavior, premature and unsafe sexual behaviors, and suicide. This list of risky behaviors looks as if it could have come from the current generation of teens, or any generation in the recent past. Adults today can remember making choices about abusing illegal drugs and alcohol, about engaging in unsafe sexual behaviors, and even about suicide. However, adults know something else: Teens facing these challenges now are, in many cases, doing so with fewer resources to support them. This reality makes the availability of Safe Sanctuaries for youth ministry ever more crucial. The Gallup Organization, in the research mentioned on page 12, found that youth involved with congregations were more likely to choose abstinence from alcohol and drugs, more likely to abstain from unsafe sexual behaviors, and less likely to attempt suicide. The significance of this relationship is further illustrated by the Gallup research. The 1992 poll indicates that alcohol use and abuse was a problem in thirty percent of the teens' families. In 1993, the National Center for Health Statistics reported that suicide is the second leading cause of death among children and youth under twenty-one years of age. Additionally, it was estimated that for every completed suicide, there are fifty to one hundred attempted adolescent suicides. The National School Safety Center reports that crimes against children and youth at school include approximately 282,000 students who are physically attacked in our secondary schools each month.

In today's world, it would be nearly impossible for any of us not to hear about incidents of abuse and violence against youth. Most abusers are people known by the teen victims. The vast majority of abusers are adults on whom the victims are physically and emotionally dependent. As recently as 2000, three million incidents of abuse were reported in the United States. As shocking as that number is, those three million reported incidents actually involved nearly five million children and youth. Child advocacy experts estimate that six million more incidents go unreported each year. Such incidents happen all too frequently, with each day bringing new horrors to light. Although abuse and violence against youth has existed in Atlanta (where I live) and probably in every community for a long time, I have observed several trends that are fairly recent developments. First, there is considerably more news coverage of such abuse and incidents of violence. Second, there is more and more effective prosecution, at local, state, and federal levels, of crimes against children and youth. Third, there are almost daily reports of abuse and violence perpetrated against youth in churches by people known, trusted, and respected by the victims. Fourth, victims of such abuse in churches, and their families and advocates, are more and more willing to seek redress

Notes:

THE GALLUP ORGANIZATION found that youth involved with congregations were more likely to choose abstinence from alcohol and drugs, more likely to abstain from unsafe sexual behaviors, and less likely to attempt suicide.

Notes:

WE MUST RECOGNIZE THAT our efforts to protect the youth will also protect adults who work with youth.

through cooperating with criminal prosecutions or pursuing litigation against the perpetrators and the churches.

News coverage of abuse against youth in the recent past has included stories of priests and other clergy abusing teens in their churches, a youth director abusing a teenager on the bus used for youth group transportation, a recreation director molesting adolescent participants in the church's sports program, and a church camp counselor sexually abusing a camper. This list is not exhaustive; it is merely illustrative of the undeniable fact that we must work harder than ever before to protect the youth in our care, recognizing that whatever efforts we have made up to this day have been only a beginning. We must also recognize that our efforts to protect the youth will also protect adults who work with youth.

Most congregations I am familiar with do well at providing ministries for the youth that will increase their faith, such as Sunday school, Bible study, confirmation studies, and other educational settings. Most congregations also do well at providing ministries for perfecting the youth in love through service projects, fellowship opportunities, mission trips, retreats, and other such settings. What about confirming their hope? How does your congregation address this facet of its responsibility for youth? In just a few short sentences, we have demonstrated that today's world is frequently an unfriendly and dangerous place for teens. Youth face the possibility of violence and abuse at home, at school, on the street, and everywhere else. Nevertheless, the youth who are connected to a community of faith seem to have greater strength with which to face these difficult circumstances. They seem to have more coping skills and a larger measure of optimism that today's hardships are not the end. In other words, they are more hopeful that today's situation, whether it is parental abuse, random violence, or anything else, is temporary and the future will be healthful and good. I believe the explanation for this is that the youth involved with a community of faith have been blessed by their interactions with, and relationships to, a number of nurturing, caring, compassionate adult leaders who over time have modeled a Christian approach to daily life. In light of the facts and statistics cited here, as well as the constant stream of media reports, we can conclude that providing youth ministries in Safe Sanctuaries not only reduces the risk of abuse within the church but will also equip the youth with the faith and hope they need to face the present and the future.

The full spectrum of the problem of abuse and violence against youth is far too broad to be comprehensively addressed here. For our purposes, we must limit our focus to the prevention of abuse in the church and its ministries. Acknowledging our limited focus does not mean there is not a lot to consider. The gospel message clearly calls our communities of faith to engage in ministries with youth that are nurturing, sustaining, and compassionate. Our society needs our communities of faith to surround youth with steadfast love so that they can be strong in the face of difficult challenges and choices. Planning for Safe Sanctuaries in youth ministries requires us to focus on at least three groups: youth, workers with youth, and the church as a whole congregation. Planning for youth includes planning for junior highs, middle highs, and senior highs. Planning for the workers with youth includes planning for pastors, youth ministers and directors, youth Sunday school teachers, youth group counselors, youth music workers, camp directors and staff members, retreat leaders, and even those who substitute when the regular workers cannot be present. Planning for the congregation includes planning for the board of trustees, the staff-parish committee, and many others.

Types of Abuse Against Youth

Generally, abuse is categorized in five primary forms: physical abuse, emotional abuse, neglect, sexual abuse, and ritual abuse. The resolution passed by General Conference calls all congregations to work to prevent all of these forms of abuse. Although we may typically think of young children when we think of these forms of abuse, youth can be victims of each and every one of these abuses.

1. **Physical Abuse**
   This is abuse in which a person deliberately and intentionally causes bodily harm to a youth or young child. Examples may include violent battery with a weapon (such as a knife or belt), burning, choking, fracturing bones, and other nonaccidental injuries.

2. **Emotional Abuse**
   This is abuse in which a person exposes a youth or younger child to spoken and/or unspoken violence or emotional cruelty. Emotional abuse sends a message to the youth that he or she is worthless, bad, unloved, and undeserving of love and care. Youth exposed to emotional abuse may have experienced being deprived of all parental affection, being locked in closets or other confining spaces, being incessantly told they are bad, or being forced to abuse alcohol or illegal drugs. This type of abuse is difficult to prove and is devastating to the victim.

Notes:

YOUTH MINISTRIES IN SAFE sanctuaries not only reduces the risk of abuse but will also equip the youth with the faith and hope they need to face the present and the future.

15

Notes:

3. **Neglect**

This is abuse in which a person endangers a youth's health, welfare, and safety through negligence. It may include withholding food, medical care, affection, and even education to destroy the youth's sense of self-esteem and self-worth. Neglect may well be the most common form of abuse. Although it is often difficult to prove, reports of neglect from teenagers should not be ignored.

4. **Sexual Abuse**

This type of abuse occurs when sexual contact between a youth and an adult (or older, more powerful youth) happens. The youth victim is not capable of consenting to such contact or resisting such sexual acts. Often, the youth victim is physically dependent on the perpetrator (for example, a parent). Additionally, the youth victim is often psychologically dependent on the perpetrator (for example, a teacher or a youth minister). Examples of sexual abuse include fondling, intercourse, incest, and the exploitation of and exposure to pornography and/or prostitution.

5. **Ritual Abuse**

This is abuse in which physical, sexual, or psychological violence is inflicted on a youth, intentionally and in a stylized way, by someone (or multiple people) with responsibility for the victim's welfare. Typically, the perpetrator appeals to some higher authority or power to justify his or her abuses. Examples of ritual abuse may include cruel treatment of animals or repetitious threats of sexual or physical violence to the youth victim or to people related to the youth victim. When reports of ritual abuse are made, they are often extremely horrifying. Such reports may even seem too gruesome to be true. However, any youth making such a report must not be ignored.

It Can Happen Anywhere

When a youth reports that he or she has experienced the behaviors detailed in these descriptions, serious attention should be paid to the report. While not every teenager's story is actually a report of abuse, the truth needs to be determined to prevent both further harm to the youth and further false allegations.

Abuse of a youth or child is criminal behavior and is punished severely in every state. Although each state has its own specific legal definition, sexual abuse exploits and harms youth by involving them in sexual behavior for which they are unprepared, to which they cannot consent, and from which they are unable to protect themselves.

WHAT IS ABUSE?

Abuse may include

–Physical abuse

–Emotional abuse

–Neglect

–Sexual Abuse

–Ritual Abuse

The youth victim is never responsible for causing the abuse and should never be blamed for it. The youth victim is not capable of consent to abusive behavior, either legally or morally. Sexual abuse of youth is always wrong and is solely the responsibility of the abuser. In some instances, the abuser who is confronted will respond defensively, saying things like, "What abuse? She wanted it!" or "What abuse? He needed some love, and I provided it." Responses such as these must not distract us from the fact that the victim was quite likely dependent on the abuser in some way and unable to defend him or herself against the acts of the abuser. For example, the victim is a student who is afraid that rejecting the teacher or coach will lead to repercussions in class or on the team. Another unfortunate but not uncommon scenario is a youth who is singled out by a youth minister or counselor for special attention. In the event the abuse is reported, the abuser's initial response may be something like, "I would never abuse one of my youth. She was having a rough time at home, and I was just trying to help." Another common response is, "He needed a loving relationship to learn about God's love, and I helped show him God's will." Needless to say, abuse of youth is never a reflection of or an incarnation of God's will in the Christian faith. Furthermore, such a claim is not, and should not be, a successful defense to an accusation of abuse.

The church must work to assure youth and families that abuse will not be tolerated or ignored in the community of faith. The church can demonstrate its commitment to providing a safe, secure place where all youth can grow in faith and wisdom by seriously addressing the need to develop and implement abuse prevention policies and strategies for every congregation. Over the past few years, United Methodist congregations have made significant progress in developing such strategies, with specific emphasis on children's ministries. Today, the time has come to go a step further and develop appropriate strategies for prevention of abuse of our youth.

Frequently, when congregations are first considering the task of developing a youth abuse prevention policy and strategy, one or more members may respond, "Well, this is silly. Such a horrible thing would never happen in our church!" Or, "I think we're blowing this issue out of proportion. Just because it happens in the big city churches doesn't mean it would ever happen here." Or, "We never have as many volunteer leaders for Sunday school and UMYF as we need. If we start making each worker answer a lot of questions and sign a covenant, we will scare everybody off. Then what will we do?" Or, "I don't see much point in this, since the youth don't come to the church often, anyway."

Notes:

THE YOUTH VICTIM IS NEVER responsible for causing the abuse and should never be blamed for it.

Notes:

Comments such as these demonstrate not only our reluctance to admit that tragedies of abuse are real for many teenagers but also our complete abhorrence of the thought that such crimes could happen in our churches, our holiest of places. Perhaps comments of this nature reveal our unfailing optimism that atrocities cannot happen in *our* church.

When the work of devising abuse prevention strategies is underway, members will inevitably learn that no church is immune from the horrors of abuse simply because it wants to be. As the work progresses, they may hear about an incident in the church across the street; or a member of the congregation will reveal that he or she is a survivor of childhood abuse; or a youth's parent will report a suspected incident of abuse to the pastor. In any of these events, the congregation's work will suddenly take on a new, more urgent, and deeper sense of importance.

Knowing the Facts

When abuse occurs in our own neighborhoods, it gets our attention and sometimes serves as a catalyst in a way that nameless and faceless teenagers counted in statistics cannot. However, it is important to know a few statistics:

- Childhelp USA, one of the largest and oldest nonprofit organizations dedicated to the treatment and prevention of child abuse, reports that in 2000 approximately three million children were reported for child abuse and neglect to child protective service agencies in the United States. This number represents children and youth through the age of eighteen. (These statistics were compiled from the U.S. Department of Health and Human Services, Children's Bureau.) Furthermore, the three million reported incidents actually involved the welfare of approximately five million children under the age of eighteen. By some estimates, the actual incidence of abuse may be three times greater than the number of incidents reported to authorities.
- Studies have estimated that one out of three girls is sexually abused before the age of eighteen. Similarly, one out of seven boys has been sexually abused before the age of eighteen. Even more frightening is that these numbers may be underestimated, since many youth are reluctant to report abuse.
- Childhelp USA also reports that approximately 1,200 deaths attributable to child abuse and/or neglect occur each year. This number includes deaths of youth attributed to physical abuse, sexual abuse, neglect, and emotional abuse; however, most of the children who die

NO CHURCH IS IMMUNE
from the horrors of abuse
simply because it wants to be.

are under the age of six. That number of deaths equates to more than three children and youth dying each day.

Let's think again about the first number listed: 3,000,000 incidents of abuse per year. That equals 8,219 youth or children abused each day; 342 abused per hour; nearly 6 (5.7) abused every minute; and one abused every 10 seconds of every hour of every day, including the sabbath.

The Church at Risk

In light of statistics such as these, it seems that any church involved with youth is a place where abuse could occur. What makes the risk for churches especially high? Several of the following factors can be named:

- Churches generally act as organizations with a high level of trust in their members, relying on the members and leaders to conduct themselves following the example of Christ. Sometimes this trusting attitude persists even in the face of questions or reports of misconduct.
- Churches are famously passive, and even inactive, when it comes to screening the volunteers and/or employees who work with youth. Often, no investigation is done at all before total strangers are welcomed aboard as new volunteer leaders.
- Churches routinely provide opportunities for close contact and close personal relationships with youth. Such relationships are sometimes encouraged without giving the workers sufficient education and training on establishing and maintaining healthy and appropriate interpersonal boundaries with the youth.

Simultaneously with the growth of the church's need for greater numbers of workers with youth, there has been an explosion in litigation against the church for incidents of sexual abuse of youth and for claims of clergy sexual misconduct. Every state now has strong statutory requirements in place for the reporting of an incident of abuse. This, coupled with the unrelenting attention focused by the media on the teenage victims and the church, has increased the number of criminal charges against the accused perpetrators of abuse as well as the number of civil lawsuits seeking monetary damages for the injuries suffered by the young victims. These civil lawsuits often name multiple defendants, including the accused perpetrator, the local church where the accused perpetrator was an employee or volunteer, and the annual conference. In lawsuits such as these, the victim (plaintiff) generally claims that one individual sexually abused him or her and that the church and/or the annual

Notes:

THREE MILLION INCIDENTS OF abuse are reported each year. That equates to one incident every ten seconds around the clock, seven days a week.

Notes:

conference was negligent in hiring and supervising the individual abuser, thus increasing the possibility that the youth would be injured.

The concept of charitable immunity, which in the past shielded churches from many types of litigation, no longer serves as a viable protection in cases of abuse or sexual misconduct. In the past, our society afforded immunity from lawsuits to organizations such as churches that were seen to be providing charitable services to the community. In other words, the churches were protected from lawsuits because their value to society as a whole was seen to be more important that any individual's possible claims of injury. Today, the public and the courts consider the harm done by abuse of youth or children too great to allow such incidents to go unreported and unpunished. Frequently, the punishment comes in the form of monetary damages in huge verdicts against the perpetrator and/or the institution in which the perpetrator worked or volunteered. These damage awards range from thousands to many millions of dollars. Often, the trial jury awards an amount far exceeding the value of the church's insurance coverage, leaving the church in danger of not being able to continue in ministry. While a church cannot guarantee the safety of every person within its community and ministries, every church can be responsible for reducing and eliminating circumstances that could lead to harm or injury.

Recognizing and understanding the frequency of the occurrence of abuse of youth and children is only part of the task. In each local congregation, we must know how to recognize indicators of possible abuse and learn ways to safely carry out our ministries without unnecessarily or unwittingly providing opportunities for abusers to harm youth. In addition, we must understand the requirements of state laws for reporting suspected incidents of abuse and develop a plan for following these requirements when the need arises.

THE CONCEPT OF CHARITABLE immunity, which in the past shielded churches from many types of litigation, no longer serves as a viable protection in cases of abuse or sexual misconduct.

The church must not look upon the reality of abuse of youth as a reason to withdraw from its ministries with youth. More than ever before, the youth in our communities need strong leadership from Christian role models to equip them with spiritual strength to face everyday challenges in school, at work, and in social arenas. We must work to assure that our ministries are carried out in responsibly safe circumstances. We, as members of the community of faith, are called to remember the pledge we have made as each child is baptized and each youth is confirmed. Remembering that, we are called to make the church a safe and holy place where youth will be strengthened in their faith and nurtured into healthy young adults.

Indicators of Youth Ab[...]

Teens suffering abuse often do [...]
therefore, it is important to be ab[...]
of abuse. The following character[...]
abuse, although they are not nece[...]
any one of the indicators may be a[...]
more or less serious problems. Whe[...]
observed in a youth, they can be co[...]
lead you to look into the situation fu[...]

Possible Signs of Physical Abuse
1. Hostile and aggressive behavior t[...]
2. Fearfulness of parents and/or othe[...]
3. Destructive behavior toward self, o[...]
   property;
4. Burns, facial injuries, pattern of repe[...]

Possible Signs of Emotional Abuse
1. Severe depression and/or withdrawal;
2. Severe lack of self-esteem;
3. Threatening or attempting suicide;
4. Eating and/or speech disorders;
5. Going to extremes to seek adult approval;
6. Extreme passive/aggressive behavior patter[...]

Possible Signs of Neglect
1. Pattern of inappropriate dress for climate;
2. Begging or stealing food/chronic hunger;
3. Depression;
4. Untreated medical conditions;
5. Poor hygiene.

Possible Signs of Sexual Abuse
1. Unusually advanced sexual knowledge and/or behavior for teen's age and developmental stage;
2. Depression—cries often for no apparent reason;
3. Promiscuous behavior;
4. Running away from home and refusing to return;
5. Difficulty walking or sitting;
6. Bruises/bleeding in vaginal or anal areas;
7. Frequent headaches, stomachaches, extreme fatigue;
8. Sexually transmitted diseases.

In addition to these indicators, youth who have been sexually abused at church may exhibit some of the following:
1. Unusual nervousness or anxiety about going to the Sunday school class alone;

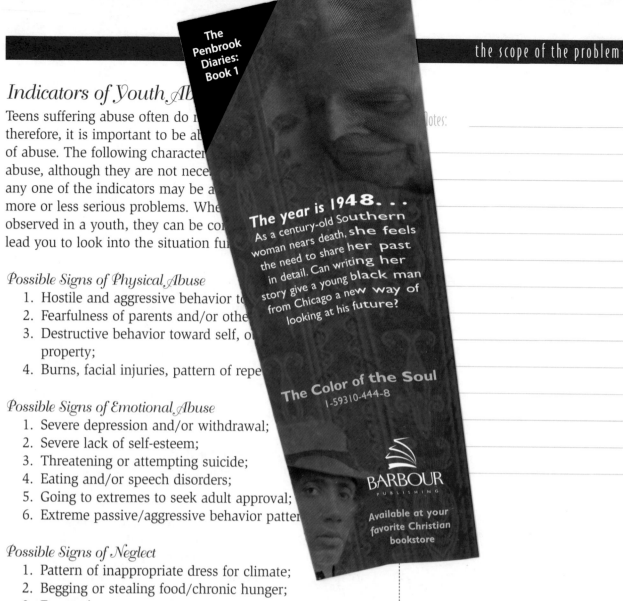
Notes:

WHILE A CHURCH CANNOT guarantee the safety of every person, every church can be responsible for reducing and eliminating circumstances that could lead to harm or injury.

Notes:

2. Reluctance to participate in church activities that were previously enthusiastically approached;
3. Comments such as "I don't want to be alone with _____," in reference to a Sunday school teacher or youth group counselor;
4. Nightmares involving a youth group adult leader or a Sunday school teacher as a frightening character;
5. Unexplained hostility toward a youth group adult leader or teacher.

Possible Signs of Ritual Abuse
1. Disruptions of memory or consciousness;
2. Unexplained mistrust and mood swings;
3. Flashbacks;
4. Eating disorders;
5. Fear of the dark, especially at sundown or a full moon;
6. Agitation, anxiety, or despair that seems to occur in cycles;
7. Fear of ministers, priests, or others wearing robes or uniforms;
8. Nightmares or sleep disorders;
9. Any of the symptoms of sexual abuse.

Abuse of youth and children occurs every minute of every day, in every community. Such abuse occurs in every economic, racial, ethnic, religious, or other demographic group. No segment of our society is immune or untouched. As Christians, we are called to be vigilant in protecting the youth in our midst and in preventing abuse in the community of faith. For many congregations, this will seem to be an impossible task. However, there are certain specific actions that can be easily taken, and with appropriate planning they will enable the congregation to move forward in providing Safe Sanctuaries for its youth ministries. These plans and actions are detailed in the following chapters.

Abusers: Who Are They?

To prevent the abuse of youth in our churches, we must not only recognize the signs of abuse but also realize that the abusers of our youth are more often than not familiar adults who are trusted by the youth. Less than twenty percent of abuse of youth is perpetrated by strangers. In other words, in more than three quarters of the reported incidents of abuse, the victim is related to or acquainted with the abuser.

Youth victims of sexual abuse and the people who abuse them come from all segments of our society. Abusers can be found in every racial, ethnic, economic, and social group.

TEENS SUFFERING ABUSE often do not tell anyone about it; therefore, it is important to recognize other signs of abuse.

They look much like us. Abusers can be charismatic leaders, especially those who work or volunteer with youth. They are sociable and willing to include the youth in their adult social events, and some are sympathetic to troubled teens. Some are married and have children, and some are unmarried; some are young, and some are older adults. Within my community in recent years, abusers have been identified as a youth detention center chaplain, foster parents, teachers, coaches, a church recreation ministry director, youth ministers, and pastors. In other words, the variety is unlimited.

Who are the abusers within our churches? They may be Sunday school teachers, camp counselors, youth group counselors, clergy, or anyone else with unlimited and unsupervised access to youth.

How Does Abuse Happen?

Sexual abuse of youth happens when a person exerts his or her power over a youth in ways that harm and/or exploit the youth. Another way of thinking about it is that the abuser is powerful because he or she has many more resources than the victim, and the youth is vulnerable perhaps in several ways. The abuser gains power over the youth victim using multiple sources: size, position, knowledge, money, just to name a few. All of these things work to make the abuser believe that he or she is able to behave abusively toward a youth and that the victim will be unable to repel or stop the abusive behavior. If the victim is physically smaller and weaker, intellectually less mature, and economically dependent on the abuser for sustenance, the abuser can readily take advantage of those circumstances. When a teen's vulnerability and an abuser's misuse of power combine with the opportunity to exploit the teen without being discovered, sexual abuse may, and often does, occur. Ministries planned and designed to minimize the possibilities of isolation of individual teens and opportunities for adult leaders to demand secrecy will provide greater protection for the youth and the workers.

Members of our churches do not like to think that any person in the Sunday school or any other ministry of the church would harm any of the youth. Conversely, we do not like to think that false allegations of abuse could be made by any youth in the church. But without a comprehensive strategy against abuse, we are taking a needless risk that harm may be done to our youth and our workers with youth.

It is imperative for our churches not to adopt or implement abuse prevention policies that apply to only a few categories

WHO ARE ABUSERS?

Abusers are not easily recognizable, for they may look just like you or me. Abusers are people who have greater power in relation to a youth, and they use that power to harm the youth.

Notes:

of people. Strategies must be supported by the whole congregation and carried out by applying the same policies and requirements to each worker involved in youth ministries, including the clergy. When a congregation adopts an abuse prevention strategy that applies only to the paid youth workers or only to professional staff members, it is doomed to be no more than partially successful. It exempts too many people from the strategy's requirements and may create specific opportunities for abusers to have unlimited access to youth.

Consequences of Sexual Abuse of Youth

When one youth is sexually abused within our church, many victims are created, including the youth, the youth's family, the congregation, and the family of the abuser. For example, if the youth minister sexually abuses a girl in the middle-high youth group and the girl reports the abuse, she may be physically injured and traumatized. She may also be doubted by others who do not want to believe such a thing could have happened. Her family will be outraged, frightened, and possibly doubted by others in the faith community. The congregation itself will likely divide into factions comprised of those who believe the youth and those who believe the accused abuser. Such divisions have been known to last for years. Finally, the abuser's family may suffer devastating consequences as a result of the loss of income and the possibility that the abuser will be sentenced to prison.

Of foremost importance is the youth who has been harmed; he or she must be cared for. Innocence has been stolen from the victim. The trauma of abuse may cause emotional injury as well as physical injury, and these scars will last through the victim's life. When sexual abuse is perpetrated by a trusted person in the church, even greater harm is done to the teen's faith in God and faith in the church. The victim may struggle with questions: If God loves everyone, how could God have let this happen to me? How can the members of this congregation continue praying and singing week after week, acting as if nothing has happened? For youth, this is a common and strong reaction. Experiences of abuse in the church create massive obstacles to a teen victim's development of a living, sustaining faith. Since this abuse occurs at the time when the youth is likely to be exploring the importance of making a lifetime faith commitment, this abuse can destroy the youth's desire to participate in the community of faith. This consequence is no less important than the physical injuries or the eventual depression, fear, and lack of sufficient self-esteem that often develop as a result of sexual abuse. For the individual victim and for the community of faith, this result is devastating.

WITHOUT A COMPREHENSIVE strategy against abuse, we are taking a needless risk that harm may be done to our youth and our workers with youth.

The congregation also becomes a victim after abuse is revealed. Members are stunned that such a crime could have been perpetrated within their midst and are humiliated at their failure to maintain the church as a safe sanctuary for youth. Members fear that they are ill equipped to help the teen's healing process. They are angry that a person welcomed into their fellowship would dare to disregard the gospel's mandate by abusing any of the youth. Often, members are divided when the congregation begins to think about how to address all of the problems created by the incident. They agonize over how to develop strategies for safety and how to provide the ministries of healing and nurture to the victim and the victim's family.

In addition, the congregation may suffer for a long time when civil or criminal litigation ensues as a result of the abuse. Litigation in the courts can keep the incident alive for months, even years, and may make resolution of the emotional issues even more difficult. Within the past year, we have seen daily news reports of the consequences and costs of civil and criminal litigation involving churches and clergypersons accused of sexual abuses. A growing trend toward criminal prosecution of abusers can be observed in the cases reported in the past year. When convictions result, the sentences often range from ten years to life in prison for the defendant. However, we cannot yet say that the trend toward criminal prosecutions is reducing the number of civil lawsuits being pursued against the churches for claims of negligent hiring, retention, or supervision. Currently, in one denomination there is such a huge number of claims pending that the denomination has let it be known that financial bankruptcy is a distinct possibility. The pending criminal prosecutions and civil suits, along with a possible bankruptcy proceeding, will quite possibly consume the resources of this church for the foreseeable future. In the meantime, the congregations will suffer as resources for ministry decline and confidence in leadership erodes. Ultimately, such a situation may lead not only to financial bankruptcy but also to a spiritual bankruptcy that would be even more difficult to recover from than financial ruin. As a result of many reports and situations like these, we have finally become aware of the effects of the long, time-consuming, and costly litigation process on the congregations and the annual conferences.

Another costly effect of sexual abuse in church has developed since the tragedy of September 11, 2001. Specifically, the insurable losses resulting from the events on that date combined with the flood of claims regarding sexual abuse in churches during 2001 and 2002 have forced some insurance

Notes:

ABUSE IN THE CHURCH
creates many victims:
- the youth
- the youth's family
- the congregation
- the family of the abuser

Notes:

companies to notify their insured churches that the company cannot continue to provide coverage for claims of sexual abuse of youth and children and for clergy sexual misconduct claims. If the company has not cancelled such coverage outright, they have probably reduced the dollar value of the coverage and required the church to present a comprehensive risk-management plan before continuing to provide such coverage.

Although criminal or civil litigation is often necessary in such situations, the litigation process itself will not provide what is needed for healing among the congregation's members. For this healing, the community of faith must dig deeply into its biblical foundations and find strength to conquer the evils of fear and the lack of knowledge about abuse. The congregation must make a renewed commitment to living out the gospel's call to provide continuing opportunities for the youth to grow in faith.

Finally, the financial consequences of sexual abuse in the church cannot be ignored. As reports of abuse and lawsuits increase, the financial costs rise exponentially. A victim of sexual abuse and his or her family will suffer financially, since the costs of counseling and medical treatment go up each year. A congregation need only ask its insurance agent for the latest statistics to learn that the amounts paid by churches, as settlements or verdicts in abuse cases, can be astronomical—ranging from thousands to millions of dollars. Even for churches that have never faced a claim or lawsuit over sexual abuse, the cost of insurance for such claims has risen dramatically in the past year. According to the Non-Profit Risk Management Center, premium costs for this type of insurance have risen anywhere from ten percent to one hundred percent for insured churches.

No congregation can afford—either financially, ethically, or morally—to fail to implement strategies for the reduction and prevention of sexual abuse of its youth. We, as Christians, are not called to discontinue our congregations' ministries with children and youth. We are called to engage in these ministries with enthusiasm and with the knowledge that we are making every effort to provide ministry to our youth in ways that assure their safety while they grow in sustaining faith.

THE CONGREGATION MAY
suffer for a long time when civil or criminal litigation ensues as a result of the abuse.

Recruiting, Screening, and Hiring Workers With Youth

WHEN A CONGREGATION decides to develop and implement a comprehensive strategy for the prevention of sexual abuse, the best place to begin is with the development of appropriate procedures for recruiting, screening, and hiring the people who will work with youth. In spite of other adopted safety procedures, if a church does not include a thorough screening process, it will not provide the control and security necessary to assure the safety of youth participating in its ministries. Every congregation can approach the recruiting/screening/hiring process in two stages. First, there needs to be a procedure for the employees and volunteers who will work with youth on a regular and frequent basis. Second, there needs to be a procedure for workers and volunteers who will be involved with youth only occasionally. By implementing such a system, even workers who are called at the last minute to replace a regular worker can be recruited from a group that has been adequately screened in advance. This can be highly valuable when planning a retreat or a mission trip for your youth group.

From the standpoint of reducing the legal liability of the church if an incident of abuse occurs, implementing a thorough screening process for the church's workers with youth and applying that process to all workers (paid and volunteer, clergy and lay) will go a long way toward demonstrating that the church has taken reasonable actions to protect its youth. Using a thorough screening process coupled with the regular use of additional safety procedures, such as the two-adult rule and open-door counseling (discussed later in this resource), demonstrates further the reasonableness of the church's actions. In addition, use of a thorough recruiting and screening process may reduce the risk of false allegations being made against youth workers. By making it known to the whole congregation that all the workers with youth have been carefully selected (indeed, hand picked) for their positions, you are assuring that only workers who will put the best interests of the youth first have been selected. Thus, people who might consider making false allegations against any of the workers will have the worker's reputation and selection as additional obstacles to overcome in making the allegations credible. Unfortunately, some youth have made false allegations of abuse against teachers or youth group counselors in hopes that their parents will postpone or discontinue pending divorce or custody litigation.

Notes:

When the church's screening and hiring practices are well known, perhaps such youth will be reluctant to falsely accuse workers in the church.

Important Forms

The following items should be included in each congregation's recruiting/screening/hiring process for workers with youth:

- Position descriptions;
- Position application forms;
- Personal reference forms;
- Consent to criminal background check forms;
- Personal interview summary forms.

Samples of each of these forms are provided in this resource (pages 76–92). These are only samples, and you should modify each, in consultation with legal counsel, to meet the requirements of your church as well as the requirements of your state and local laws. The appropriate use of these forms will vary, depending on whether you are recruiting occasional workers or regular workers, both paid and volunteer workers and clergy or lay workers.

Recruiting Regular Workers

For full-time, part-time, paid, volunteer, clergy, or lay, use an application form that requests comprehensive information regarding the applicant's

- identification;
- address;
- employment history for the past five years;
- volunteer work during the past five years;
- experiences and skills specifically related to the position;
- prior church membership (if any);
- personal references (not related to applicant), with complete addresses;
- consent to verify all information provided and to contact the references;
- waiver of any right to confidentiality and of any right to pursue damages against the church caused by the references' responses;
- certification that the information provided is true and correct.

If permitted in your local legal jurisdiction, also request that the applicant list any criminal convictions (even traffic violations, since workers with youth often need to drive church vehicles).

Finally, include a space for the applicant's signature and date.

A THOROUGH RECRUITING and screening process may reduce the risk of false allegations being made against your workers.

Reference Check Forms

Forms similar to the sample on page 84 provide the church with an outline of the information needed from references, as well as a place to note the responses if the contact is being made by telephone. These forms are also useful if the reference check is conducted through the mail. Business references, such as from previous employers, tend not to be really useful because businesses tend to give only dates-of-employment information when asked for a reference.

Interviews

A personal interview is not required for every applicant but should certainly be conducted for any the church is seriously considering after reviewing the individual applications and references. Use the interview to clarify any questions you may have about information on the application and to form a firsthand impression of the applicant. It is recommended that the applicant be interviewed by more that one person, if possible. For example, if the applicant is seeking a position as youth director, a good interview team would be comprised of some of the current volunteer leaders, some of the youth, and some parents of the youth. The interview team described here could have as few as three members, or more, depending on your particular circumstances. Training for conducting this type of screening interview is often available from agencies such as the YMCA or the Girl Scouts. If training is available in your location, take advantage of it. Good interviews are thorough interviews, not simply off-the-cuff superficial conversations. Develop your basic questions in advance. Include questions such as these:

1. What are your expectations of the youth in our group?
2. Why are you seeking a leadership position with our youth group?
3. What experience have you had as a youth group leader?
4. In your opinion, what are the best characteristics of teenagers?
5. What do teenagers need to learn in youth ministry?
6. How would you describe appropriate discipline for teenagers?
7. What is your most typical response to conflict between two or more people?
8. Have you ever been arrested for, or convicted of, child abuse or any related offense? If so, please explain the circumstances.
9. Have you ever been arrested for, or convicted of, driving under the influence? If so, please explain the circumstances.

TRAINING FOR CONDUCTING this type of screening interview is often available from agencies such as the YMCA or the Girl Scouts. Take advantage of it.

Notes:

10. How would you describe your gifts for leading youth ministry?
11. How would you respond if one of the teens broke her leg on the ski trip and you were the adult leader in charge?
12. Do you have current first aid training?

Beyond these sample questions, plan to ask more-detailed questions related to the specific ministries your youth are, and will be, engaged in. In addition, remember that you can use a revised version of these questions as you conduct telephone interviews with the people listed as references.

Screening Workers

To implement the recruiting and screening procedures outlined here, it will be necessary to have the appropriate forms completed by all the workers who are already working. New applicants should be required to complete the entire procedure before being considered for a position.

Ideally, a recruiting and screening procedure like the one described here will be applied equally to any member of the church staff (paid or volunteer, clergy or lay) who will be involved in work and ministry with youth. Sometimes the clergy do not recognize the importance of following the procedures. Clergy have said things like, "Oh, you don't need to check me out. I'm a minister!" Or, "The annual conference board of ministry has already done all this; and if the board says I'm good enough for this church, then I don't have to answer any more questions."

Responses like these put the church in an awkward and difficult position. The usual result is that the church applies the screening procedures only to nonclergy workers and takes a risk on the character of the clergyperson. We certainly hope that the church does not come to regret its choice. Nevertheless, it is always necessary to remind churches that allegations of sexual abuse are brought against clergy as well as laity, especially in the arena of youth ministry. During the past year, hardly a day has passed without a new report regarding a clergyperson being accused of sexually abusing a teenage parishioner. These reports always include the details of the lawsuit being filed on behalf of the victim, including the allegations against the church for negligent hiring and supervision of the offender. If an incident involving a clergyperson who refused to submit to the screening procedure is reported, how will the church respond when the victim's parents cry, "How could you let this so-called minister be involved with our youth when he had a criminal record?"

THE CHURCH'S SCREENING procedures should be equally applied to all workers (paid or volunteer, clergy or lay) who will interact with youth.

Even if the church is able to assuage the grief of the victim's parents, the church will still face staggering consequences when litigation ensues. Beyond the financial consequences, the congregation will be confronted by haunting thoughts: *If only we had stood firm and made Rev. _____ fill out those forms.* One church suffered through the criminal trial of one of its youth ministers that ended with a conviction and a ninety-year sentence. Then, just when the congregation began to hope they could return to some level of normalcy, the church was named as a defendant in a civil lawsuit seeking monumental monetary damages on behalf of the offender's multiple youth victims. This church had in place a thorough recruiting and screening process; however, they apparently disregarded their own policies in the selection of this staff member. The congregation continues to suffer sad consequences as a result of their decisions.

If clergy do not cooperate in the screening procedures, they have little defense if false allegations are made against them. Local churches expect that their ministers are of sterling character—and they usually are. Therefore, clergy should not be overly concerned about reference and criminal background checks. Once the responses are on file, the church can prove that it made reasonable efforts to screen staff members and that no reason was discovered that would preclude the person's involvement with youth. Clergy who are concerned about providing true leadership for their congregations are ready and willing to consent to a criminal background check when they come to a new church. Why? Because that enables the clergyperson to demonstrate his or her good character from the beginning, and it enables the congregation to publicize that the entire staff, including clergy members, are highly trustworthy.

In other words, full cooperation with the screening procedure by clergy staff creates a win–win situation for the church and the clergy. The church is able to maintain the integrity of its commitment to the prevention of abuse, and the clergyperson sets a good example for all other staff. In addition, the clergyperson's good character is reinforced by the reports received from his or her references.

Recruiting Occasional Workers

Every congregation needs workers from time to time to fill in or substitute for the regular workers who are absent. The recruiting/screening procedures outlined for full-time or part-time workers are also ideal for use with workers who may substitute or volunteer for only a few hours or a few events each year. However, it is impossible in a local church to use

CLERGY WHO ARE CONCERNED about providing true leadership for their congregations are ready and willing to consent to a criminal background check.

Notes:

SCREENING REDUCES THE RISK OF

—a child abuser being recruited to work with your children.

—your church being accused of negligent hiring practices.

—false allegations being brought against workers.

such a procedure at the last minute to identify a substitute worker when a regular worker cannot come to work and the youth director says, "My middle-high Sunday school teacher is sick today. Could you fill in?" An adult is usually happy to volunteer, the youth director's problem is solved, and everyone has a good experience. Imagine the consequences if the substitute volunteer is later accused of abusing one of the youth during the Sunday school hour. Whether the accusation turns out to be true or false, a crisis is created for the church, for the youth and his or her family, and for the volunteer and his or her family.

How can the local church maintain its commitment to preventing abuse, including a thorough screening of all workers with youth, and still have enough flexibility to recruit last-minute help? One possibility is to create a bank of potential occasional volunteers by introducing the church's policies and procedures to new members in their initial membership orientation.

The new-member orientation could include
- a membership form requesting the following information: name, address, church membership during the past three to five years, volunteer work done in previous churches, and two references with addresses (if the new member is not transferring by letter from the previous church). Explain that each new member will be asked to fill out the membership form before he or she is invited to volunteer as a worker with youth, and that no new member will be invited to volunteer to work with youth before he or she has been a member of the church for at least six months.
- a written copy of the church's policies and procedures for the prevention of abuse of youth and children.
- a covenant for the member to sign stating that in the event the member is recruited to work with youth or children, he or she agrees to follow the church's policies and procedures for the prevention of abuse of youth and children.

By providing these things to each new member, you are giving members the opportunity to inform the church of their desire to work with youth. You are also giving new members the opportunity to learn the church's policies and to either cooperate with them or decide not to volunteer with youth.

This type of new-member orientation and screening serves two important purposes: It helps the congregation identify new members who are willing to volunteer with youth, and it possibly will discourage a potential abuser from any effort to abuse in this congregation. Thus, you have created another win–win situation for the youth and for the congregation.

Use of Criminal Background Checks

Using criminal background or records checks as a part of the local church's recruiting/screening/hiring process for workers with youth is the part of the process most often objected to. However, doing a criminal background check is the most important step in the recruiting process. People seeking employment, or simply volunteering to teach Sunday school, may see this as an invasion of their privacy and an affront to their integrity. Comments can be expected, including, "I've been a member of this church for years. If they don't trust me by now, they can just find someone else to work with the youth group!" Or, "What is this world coming to? All I wanted to do was help with Sunday school. What's so hard about that?"

Reactions such as these must not dissuade our congregations from using criminal background/records checks as a primary screening tool in churches. Some states require such inquiries by any organization recruiting workers with youth and children as part of the state's child abuse laws. Insurance companies commonly tell their insured churches that use of criminal background checks is an expected part of a comprehensive risk-management plan and is not to be foregone.

As your church plans its screening procedures, here are some initial questions to consider about background checks: Does your state law require its use? Will your local legal jurisdiction assist in the records check? What information is required by the law enforcement agency to perform the records check? To help your congregation gather the necessary information, it will be useful to consult a local attorney, your church's insurance agent, and local law enforcement officers.

The most frequently asked question regarding background checks is, How much will it cost the church? On average, the cost is usually about twenty-five dollars per individual. In some jurisdictions, the local law enforcement agency will perform such checks at a reduced rate for churches. In addition to local law enforcement agencies, a large number of private companies will perform background checks for a reasonable fee.

The most important question to be asked and answered about the use of background checks is, How much will it cost the church *not* to use background checks? From the perspective of legal liabilities and how the church will cope with

SOME STATES REQUIRE criminal background/records checks by any organization recruiting workers with youth and children.

Notes:

allegations of abuse perpetrated by a staff person or volunteer for whom no background check was performed, the answer is that it will cost the church astronomically more than it would have cost to run the background check. As soon as allegations of abuse are made against a church worker and it is learned that the worker had a prior criminal record, the church will begin to experience the costs of not having conducted background checks. The costs will continue to add up for the church until the investigation is completed, lawsuits are concluded, verdicts or settlements are rendered, victims are restored to health, and the community's trust in the church is renewed. In other words, the costs to the church will go on for far longer than it would have taken to conduct thorough screening of potential workers, and the costs will be far higher than twenty-five dollars.

The local church must decide what to do with the information it receives from background reports. A strict plan should be developed to ensure that information will be kept confidential and that it will be shared only with those who must know. The church will need to decide where the reports will be stored.

If information shows that an applicant was convicted of child abuse, child molestation, incest, or some other crime against a child or teenager, that applicant should definitely be rejected as a worker with children or youth. If information indicates that charges were filed against an applicant but that there was no conviction, the church should investigate to find out how the issue was resolved. Contact the police department or the prosecuting attorney's office to discover more of the details. When the maximum amount of information has been gathered, you will need to decide whether this applicant poses too great a risk to the church's youth. Be sure to document in the church's confidential file every step taken during the investigation and the decisions made. If information shows that an applicant was convicted of some other crime, such as shoplifting or a bad check, you will have to decide whether those convictions should prohibit the applicant's involvement with youth. As a general rule of thumb, it is reasonable to prohibit the placement of any applicant who has a criminal history of child-abuse-type offenses or a history of any other violent crime, such as armed robbery, rape, or any weapons and drug charges.

No form of resistance, objection, or lack of cooperation should be allowed to stop a local congregation from developing and implementing comprehensive recruiting/screening/hiring policies and procedures for all its workers with youth.

THE MOST IMPORTANT question to be asked and answered about the use of background checks is, How much will it cost the church *not* to use background checks?

No paid or volunteer, clergy or lay, full-time or part-time workers with youth should be exempted from the screening process. If any stranger, new member, or worker can have immediate access to youth, the effect of any other safety procedures your congregation adopts will be limited. In light of the recent events in churches across our country, which have been well documented in courts and in the media, our churches would do well to adopt strict screening procedures and then make the adopted Safe Sanctuaries policies well known throughout the entire local community. Families today are anxious to find congregations who are working to keep their youth safely and actively involved in ministry. A sample announcement of the congregation's Safe Sanctuaries policies is included among the forms in this book (page 77).

Notes:

IF ANY STRANGER, NEW member, or worker can have immediate access to youth, the effect of any other safety procedures will be limited.

Notes: _____

_____

_____

_____

_____

_____

_____

_____

_____

_____

_____

_____

_____

Outline Your New Plans for Recruiting and Screening Youth Workers

1.

2.

3.

4.

5.

Basic Procedures for Safe Ministry With Youth

AFTER A LOCAL CHURCH has made the commitment to take precautions against abuse in its ministries with youth and developed its basic Safe Sanctuaries policy statement, the congregation needs to develop basic procedures to guide the day-to-day operation of its ministries. This brings us to the nuts and bolts of carrying out the church's ministries with youth after the workers are chosen. The Safe Sanctuaries procedures are designed to make ministry flow smoothly by reducing the possibility of harm to the youth and to the workers with youth. Once again, the procedures will demonstrate to members and visitors the church's commitment to the prevention of abuse of youth as well as its commitment to being a safe and holy place where youth will grow in the faith they so much need to sustain them in today's world.

Each of the following procedures is important in the congregation's comprehensive prevention strategy. They are not listed in order of importance.

Appropriate Interpersonal Boundaries

Youth ministry can be described by many adjectives, but the first one is almost always *relational*. Youth get involved, and stay involved, with youth ministries because the ministries offer opportunities to experience relationships with peers and adults that are healthy, both physically and spiritually. Whether they can articulate this or not, the youth want and need to see good examples from the adult leaders of appropriate ways to relate to others. Adults who model respectful and nurturing behaviors that do not interfere with another's privacy provide these types of good examples. The youth will follow the lead of the adults in this regard; therefore, it is important for the adult workers to be clear about appropriate behaviors. Adult workers must be attentive to appropriate dress codes (some groups have found it effective to adopt actual dress codes for retreats, trips, and regular meetings), appropriate use of language, and appropriate demonstrations of affection and encouragement. A good rule of thumb for adult leaders is to never initiate a hug and to always be the one to end the hug. A retired junior high and high school educator put it this way, "If it's not yours, don't touch it." In other words, offer hugs when they are

Notes:

requested, but do not ever impose your touches on the youth in your group. Whenever a question arises about where to draw appropriate interpersonal boundaries, remember that you are the adult and it is your responsibility to behave professionally, even if you are a volunteer.

The Two-Adult Rule

Simply stated, the two-adult rule requires no fewer than two adults present at all times during any church-sponsored program, event, or ministry involving youth. Risk will be reduced even more if the two adults are not related. The Sunday school class is always attended by at least two adults. A Bible study group for youth is always taught by at least two adults. The youth fellowship group is always staffed with at least two adult counselors/leaders.

The significance of this rule cannot be overstated. A church will drastically reduce the possibility of an incident of abuse if this rule is followed. Abusers thrive on secrecy, isolation, and their ability to manipulate their victims. When abusers know they will never have a chance to be alone with potential victims, they quickly lose interest in working with youth. Thus, the youth are protected, and the church has greatly reduced the likelihood of a claim that abuse has been perpetrated by one of its volunteers or workers and reduced the likelihood of a claim of negligence against the church. Furthermore, vigilant adherence to the two-adult rule provides important protection to the church's workers with children and youth. Even small churches can adhere to this rule by using assigned adult roamers, volunteers who move in and out of classrooms and recreation areas and function as additional helpers. Parents and youth who know that two adults will be present at all times are less likely to make false allegations, since it would be nearly impossible to prove allegations against two workers. Church members will be more confident when they volunteer to work with youth, because they will know that they will never bear the total burden of leadership and that the church has made a commitment to protecting them as well as the youth.

First Aid/CPR Training

Providing first aid and CPR training on an annual basis for all church workers with youth is a basic step to assure the safety of youth. Of course, we all hope that first aid or CPR would never be needed in the church. Nevertheless, ministries with youth inevitably involve activities that can result in bumps, bruises, scrapes, or worse. Having workers who are prepared to deal with these competently goes a long way

A CHURCH WILL DRASTICALLY reduce the possibility of an incident of abuse by following the two-adult rule.

toward building the confidence of the youth and parents involved in the ministry of the church. In youth ministry, first aid competency is crucial on every trip, whether the group is going on a ski retreat or a mission project. Over the past four years, my church's senior-high youth group has gone on a ski trip each January. On each trip prior to this year, at least one youth skier was injured. The injuries ranged from bruises to concussions to broken bones. This year, one of the adult leaders broke his wrist. Adult leaders with good first aid training were a blessing on these trips.

Annual Orientation for Workers

All workers with youth—whether paid or volunteer, part-time or full-time, clergy or lay—should be required to attend an orientation session in which they are informed of the
- church's policies for the prevention of the abuse of youth;
- procedures to be used in all ministries with youth;
- appropriate steps to follow for reporting an incident of abuse of any of the youth;
- details of your state's laws regarding the definitions of child/youth abuse and the requirements of reporting abuse when it is discovered.

At this orientation the workers are given an opportunity to renew their covenant to abide by and cooperate with the church's policies and procedures. The church will have an updated record that it has informed all of its workers about its policies. Workers who do not attend should be contacted and asked to renew the covenant. The rate of turnover among workers with youth is high; therefore, you may find it prudent to offer this type of training every six months.

The Five-Years-Older Rule

Often, especially in youth ministry, the people who volunteer to work with or who apply for a paid position are in college or have just graduated from college. If a junior in college (age twenty or twenty-one) is recruited as a counselor in the senior-high youth fellowship, the counselor may be leading youth who are only three or four years younger than he or she is. This should be prohibited for the protection of the youth and of the worker. Nearly every church has members who can remember a situation in which this rule was not followed and the people involved came to regret it. Do not make the same mistake. College students might be successful as workers with the junior-high youth, or the middle-high group; but they should not be given the sole responsibility for any group.

Notes:

PROVIDING FIRST AID AND CPR training on an annual basis for all church workers with youth is a basic step to assure the safety of youth.

Notes:

No Workers Under the Age of Eighteen

When a church implements this rule, it goes a long way toward reducing the risks of injuries to its youth. A common practice in churches is to allow junior- and senior-high-aged volunteers in the church nursery. I have known of a church who used the junior-high youth to staff the infant nursery as a service project for the church. In effect, the church used children to supervise children. While in some situations they may provide excellent help, people under the age of eighteen cannot be expected to have developed the maturity and judgment that is needed to be fully responsible for younger children or younger youth. Putting children in charge of children invites disaster. Even in the context of using older youth to work with the younger group, you are taking unnecessary risks. Older youth sometimes abuse or bully their younger, smaller, and weaker peers. Many states have laws defining such behavior as child abuse and providing for significant sentences. It is not advisable or prudent to take the risk of relying on youth to lead themselves or their younger peers.

Windows in All Classroom Doors

Each room set aside for youth should have a door with a window in it or a half-door. A window in every door removes the opportunity for secrecy and isolation, conditions every abuser seeks. A half-door offers protection by offering full visual access to anyone walking by. Many pastors are adding a window in their study or office door to set a good example for the church and to protect themselves against false allegations of misconduct. Our youth need to be able to meet with one another and their adult leaders to study, worship, and fellowship in safety. Using areas that are visually accessible and classrooms that have windows in the door makes safe meetings possible by preventing would-be abusers from isolating an intended victim in a hidden or secret area.

Open-Door Counseling

At any counseling sessions with youth, the door of the room used should remain open for the entire session. Ideally, the session will be conducted at a time when others are nearby, even if they are not within listening distance. Counseling sessions conducted behind closed doors are a breeding ground for false allegations of abuse. Closed doors also make it too easy for the abuser to have the privacy and isolation he or she needs to carry out abusive acts. When one of our youth is troubled and seeks counseling, it is critical to resist the temptation to meet the youth in secret, even if the youth makes that request.

A WINDOW IN EVERY DOOR removes the opportunity for secrecy and isolation, conditions every abuser seeks.

Limited Counseling Sessions

Whenever a youth seeks counseling, it is important to determine in the initial meeting if you are actually qualified to address the youth's needs effectively. If you do not believe you are sufficiently qualified, refer the youth to another counselor. In the event you do agree to counsel the youth, it may be prudent to agree to a limited number of sessions (two or three) and then refer the youth to another counselor if the problems have not been solved. In this way, if you cannot successfully help the youth, you will at least not unduly delay the counseling process with someone else.

Advance Notice to Parents

A basic rule for ministry with youth is always to give the parents advance notice and full information regarding the event in which their youth will be participating. Risk-management officers advise clients to notify parents of any event in which a worker will be alone with a youth member of the group. Before the event, parents must give written permission for their child's participation. Doing this protects the church, in that it proves that parents were informed of the event, warned of the situation, and given the chance to prevent their youth from being alone with a worker.

Providing parents with advance notice and full information about activities must be a guiding principle in a church's ministries with youth. Advance information encourages parents to support the ministry by scheduling their youth's participation. It could also possibly lead to parents participating in the ministry as volunteer leaders. Advance information can help parents and youth decide whether the content and substance of the event are suitable for their participation. Most importantly, advance information demonstrates that the church takes its ministries seriously enough to plan thoroughly and to provide for the safest possible experiences. For example, one Sunday evening the youth group activities at my church ended a little earlier than usual. When the other teens had already been picked up by their parents, my daughter was still there waiting for me. Even though our home is almost directly behind the church property and driving from the church to our home takes only a few minutes, the assistant youth director called me to ask if I would like for him to give her a ride or if I would prefer to pick her up. This was a good decision and a demonstration of good judgment from a risk-management perspective, but it was also good because he gave me full information and let me be involved in the choice. A parent who is informed, and even consulted, will surely be a parent supportive of the youth ministry.

Notes:

PROVIDING PARENTS WITH advance notice and full information about activities must be a guiding principle in a church's ministries with youth.

Notes:

WHEN A CHURCH HAS MADE A serious commitment to a comprehensive plan for the prevention of abuse within its ministries, it will want to provide information about the plan to the congregation and parents.

Participation Covenant for All Participants and Leaders

A written covenant of participation should be developed and provided to all leaders and participants in youth ministries. The covenant is a statement in which the participants and leaders agree to

- take part in the ministry;
- give their best efforts to the ministry;
- respect the other participants;
- treat the others as well as they would wish to be treated.

Such covenants are useful (especially for retreats or trips) for establishing from the outset the behavior standards expected of everyone. The covenants are also important reminders for leaders that abusive behavior toward the youth will not be tolerated.

Parent and Family Education

When a church has made a serious commitment to a comprehensive plan for the prevention of abuse within its ministries, it will want to provide information about the plan to the congregation and parents. A family education event, or a series of events, in which families are invited to learn the facts about abuse and about the components of the church's plan is highly effective in disseminating full information to the maximum number of people in a minimum amount of time. An event of this type could include

- a speaker from your local law enforcement agency;
- a speaker from a local child protective services agency;
- a doctor or counselor who is experienced in treating abused youth;
- an attorney experienced in advising churches about risk management or loss prevention;
- a video about the incidence of sexual abuse of youth and children within churches;
- printed information about your state's abuse statutes and abuse reporting requirements;
- printed copies of your church's abuse prevention policies and procedures (allowing time for discussion);
- a time for worship and prayer.

An event like this can also include sessions for youth so that they are informed about the behavior that is to be expected from other participants and from church leaders, about appropriate interpersonal boundaries with one another and with adult leaders, about how to recognize and report possible abuse, and about how they can help prevent harm being done to anyone at the church.

In a church committed to the prevention of abuse, this event will be provided regularly to accommodate new members and new parents.

Appropriate Equipment and Supervision

Ministries with youth are carried out in an endless variety of settings and locations: church sanctuaries, classrooms, camp cabins, athletic fields, retreat centers, tour buses, parks, and homes. Reports of abuse indicate that abuse happens in an equally large variety of settings. One aspect of planning for the safety of the youth participants is arranging for the ministry to take place in an appropriate setting. For instance, if the purpose of the ministry is weekly Bible study, then an appropriate setting would be a classroom at the church. If the purpose of the ministry is for the youth choir to travel for two weeks performing a musical in a dozen different cities, then the settings may include a tour bus, a series of hotel rooms, and a series of church sanctuaries.

The likelihood of the occurrence of abuse varies in different settings and circumstances. Bible study done in an open-doored classroom and in the presence of no fewer than two adults has a low probability of an incident happening. However, inadequate supervision of a youth choir at a hotel may increase the odds of an abuse incident. It is important for those planning ministries with children and youth to think through, in advance, the advantages and disadvantages of the settings they are considering.

Ministries with youth often involve using special equipment, and workers should know how to safely operate whatever equipment is needed. For instance, the youth group at my church has a Christmas tree sale each year to earn money for their summer mission trips. This project requires the use of handsaws, chainsaws (operated only by adults), hammers, ropes, and a calculator. Without adequate adult supervision and the ability of the workers to safely operate these items, the tree sale could turn into a disaster. Many youth groups participate in athletic events, such as rock climbing, rappelling, skateboarding, softball, basketball, and football. Activities like these need specific equipment, training, and supervision.

Other outdoor ministries would involve the need for specialized knowledge. Swimming or rafting events need a supervisor with lifeguard skills. When the ministry involves camping, hiking, and service projects such as Habitat for Humanity or the Appalachian Service Project, first aid and CPR skills are needed.

Notes:

THE LIKELIHOOD OF ABUSE varies in different settings and circumstances. One aspect of planning for the safety of youth is arranging for appropriate settings.

Notes:

Adequate Insurance for the Scope of Your Ministries

Every local church needs to develop a good relationship with its insurance agent and to be adequately insured for the scope of its ministry. If the church is never involved in ministries in which people are transported in motor vehicles, then perhaps it can afford not to carry insurance for such occasions. However, for congregations involved with youth ministries, this is unlikely. Today, youth ministries need to be mobile more than ever before. Congregations, through their boards of trustees, should carefully consider all ministries and work with insurance agents to secure adequate coverage for them. Each local church that has adopted a plan for the prevention of abuse in youth ministry will be well ahead in the task of securing economical insurance coverage. If the church has not developed a plan for the prevention of such abuse, the insurance agent will be a valuable resource in supplying up-to-date information about the risks associated with abuse of youth in churches.

Youth Group Websites

Youth directors are using e-mail and youth group websites more and more to communicate with the youth group members and the parents of youth. If this is your group's practice, be prudent in the ways you use this technology. Use e-mail to communicate only information related to youth ministry, not for generally broadcasting miscellaneous generic jokes, news items, or other information. Be aware that the e-mail identity information of the group members should be protected and not be given out. If you post photos on the website, do not identify specific individuals by name. In addition, get written permission from the youth and their parents before posting photos. Use blocking tools to keep unwanted and inappropriate material from popping up on your site.

Transportation Options

It is often necessary in youth ministry to plan the best form of transportation for the project you are going to be involved in. The options often include cars, vans, and buses. Many churches have their own buses or vans that the youth group uses for trips. In such a situation, the adult leaders must be sure the vehicles are properly functioning, the church's insurance is up to date, and the adults who will be drivers are properly insured. Another possible alternative is to use commercial vehicles rented by the church and staffed with professional drivers. This option has advantages, especially if the trip is going to be a long one or you expect the traveling conditions to be hazardous. For example, you may be

USE E-MAIL TO COMMUNICATE only information related to youth ministry. The e-mail identity information of the group members should be protected and not be given out.

reasonably comfortable taking the senior highs on a weekend retreat in a couple of vans to a site only an hour or two from your church. On the other hand, if you are taking a group to a ski retreat that is five hundred miles away and the weather predictions are for snow and ice, using a commercial bus and professional driver would be a wise decision.

In the past couple of years, there have been some highly publicized accidents and wrecks involving youth groups traveling in fifteen-passenger vans. Studies have shown that these vehicles have a high propensity for rolling over. The National Highway Traffic Safety Administration has issued guidelines for operating fifteen-passenger vans more safely. The guidelines include not filling the van with more than ten passengers, not loading luggage or equipment on the top of the van, and not overloading the cargo area at the rear of the van. If your church uses such a vehicle, exercise a reasonable amount of caution.

Notes:

THE NATIONAL HIGHWAY
Traffic Safety Administration has issued guidelines for operating fifteen-passenger vans more safely.

Notes: _____

_____

_____

_____

_____

_____

_____

_____

_____

_____

_____

_____

Our Church's Insurance Coverage Includes

1.

2.

3.

4.

5.

Our First Family Education Event Includes

1.

2.

3.

4.

5.

Settings for Youth Ministries— Safe and Secure

THE PREVIOUS CHAPTER surveyed a variety of concepts and procedures for making ministries with youth more safe and secure for youth and for adults who work with them. Although most of these procedures are described in the context of using them in local church settings, they are also applicable in other youth ministry settings. Settings outside the local church may include retreats, camps, mission trips, musical and drama productions, choir trips, lock-ins, service projects, and others. Anytime a trip is being planned, review your usual procedures to be sure you will be able to implement the appropriate ones on the trip.

Several facets of a trip, or a retreat, with the youth group need special attention. These include transportation plans, interpersonal boundaries in relationships, and sleeping arrangements.

Transportation plans: Be sure you have adequate and safe transportation for the trip. Address each of the following questions: Will we be able to have each passenger in a seat belt? Will we have enough space for the passengers to be reasonably comfortable and for all the luggage and equipment? Will we have a sufficient number of drivers who are qualified? Will we have first aid supplies? Will we have a cell phone or some other way to communicate in an emergency? Will we have a map and good directions?

Interpersonal boundaries in relationships: Trips provide wonderful opportunities for fellowship and nurturing positive and affirming relationships among the youth and adults in your group. You have more time to spend together and, thus, greater opportunities to interact. Just by doing normal things, such as cooking meals and cleaning up the kitchen or working on a mission project together, the youth have more chances for conversation—more sharing of their thoughts, opinions, hopes, and dreams—than in their usual settings. This interaction may be the greatest value of trips. It may also be the source of greatest risk. Before going on a trip, both the youth and the adult leaders must think through the needs for a simple and respectful code of conduct.

Notes:

BEFORE GOING ON A TRIP, both the youth and the adult leaders must think through the needs for a simple and respectful code of conduct.

Beginning with the concept that both the youth and the leaders are expected to treat others as they would want to be treated, the leadership team can outline any other specific expectations. Modeling positive nurturing relationships might include no profane language, no practical jokes that would be physically harmful, no permission for boys to enter the room where girls are sleeping or for girls to enter the room where boys are sleeping, and no permission for two youth or one adult and one youth to separate themselves from the group. Keeping the focus on developing stronger relationships among the whole group, rather than on developing new romances, will help keep the group attentive to one another and minimize opportunities for couples to pair up.

The adults will provide great leadership by modeling appropriate behaviors. For example, adults who stay involved with the youth and in the presence of the youth, instead of pairing off or going solo away from the group, are providing good models. Adults who express affection for members of the group by hugging them in the presence of others can model affirmation for the youth without creating the perception that the personal space and privacy of the individual group member is being violated. As the leaders think about appropriate standards of conduct, the key factors to consider are that everyone should be expected to be present with the group when activities are going on and that opportunities for two youth or one adult and one youth to isolate themselves away from the group should be minimized.

Youth camping programs provide opportunities for youth to build interpersonal skills. Nearly every annual conference supports such programs, which give a large number of youth a chance to get away from their daily routines and learn profound lessons about interdependence in the community of faith. However, these ministries can also present risks for abuse. Typically, our summer camping programs are staffed by college students and young adults, which is usually safe and effective. However, the schedule should specify where staff members should be (with their camper groups or in areas reserved for staff) during lights out and other activities. In addition, the staff members should be trained to model appropriate behavior in all situations. For example, staff members should know how to respond to a request from a camper for a private conversation. In such an event, the camp staffer can offer to listen to the camper in a location where they could be seen but not heard, thus eliminating a chance for isolation of a camper and secret behavior that could be abusive. During the course of a week at camp, the campers and staff members will be involved in a wide variety of activities, from doing ordinary daily activities to hiking, swimming, camping out, playing sports, and worshiping. Through all these events, the staff members must be attentive to carrying out the activities safely and to putting the best interests of the campers first. If this is accomplished, the risk of abuse is diminished and the experience of camping will be happily remembered by the youth.

Sleeping arrangements: Today, safe sleeping plans are surely necessary when a youth group takes a trip. In days gone by, most trips were taken to church retreat centers, where all the girls slept in one large barracks-type room and all the boys slept in a similar room on the other side of the building. The female adult leaders slept in the room with the girls, and the male adult leaders slept in the room with the boys. The risks in these situations were most often a result of behavior among the members of the group.

In today's world, youth groups go on trips that require sleeping in public accommodations, such as hotels or dormitories on college campuses. Thus, the leaders must plan for minimizing the possibility of danger from within the group as well as from strangers. In addition, hotels typically provide sleeping rooms for two or four people. If four people are assigned to one hotel room, they will most likely have only two beds for the four to share. So, how can room assignments be made to maximize the safety of the youth and minimize the possibility of abuse? In a hotel-type setting, it is recommended that youth be assigned to rooms and adults be assigned to separate rooms. This would also be recommended for dormitory settings. If possible, make the room assignments so that an adult room is between two youth rooms. It is also recommended that the adults arrange among themselves to check on the youth rooms on a random schedule during the night. One youth group I know of is fortunate enough to have an adult leader who volunteers to take the night shift, staying awake and making sure there are no illicit comings and goings. Finally, if at all possible, choose a hotel where the rooms open to the interior of the building, rather than to the outside. This is crucial for minimizing the danger of strangers from the street.

It is obvious that these types of arrangements must be made carefully to protect the youth from abuse and to protect the adults from the possibility of false allegations. It may not be possible to eliminate every possibility of trouble, but prudent planning will help make things go as safely as can be reasonably expected.

Notes:

STAFF MEMBERS IN A CAMP setting should know how to respond to a request from a camper for a private conversation.

Notes: _____

_____

_____

_____

_____

_____

_____

_____

_____

_____

_____

_____

Our Weekly Ministry Settings Are

1.

2.

3.

4.

5.

Our Summer Ministry Settings Are

1.

2.

3.

4.

5.

Our Ministry Settings Are Safe Because

1.

2.

3.

4.

5.

Developing a Congregational Plan for Responding to Allegations of Abuse

THE CONGREGATION'S PLAN for responding to suspected or alleged incidents of abuse of youth must be developed long before it may be needed. Two key components must be included in the plan: First, review your state's law for requirements in reporting suspected or known incidents of abuse to child protective services or to the local police. Second, develop a plan for complying with the legal reporting requirements and for making statements to other officials, the congregation, and the media.

State Reporting Requirements

All workers with youth must know their state's requirements in reporting abuse to law enforcement authorities and child protective services. Each state has specific requirements, and you should consult a local attorney about what requirements are applicable to the workers in your church.

In some states, all workers with youth—either paid or volunteer—are mandated to report suspected cases of youth and child abuse when they have reasonable cause to believe that abuse has occurred or is occurring. However, this is not true in every state. It is imperative to know what your state requires. In some states, ordained ministers are not mandatory reporters, even if they are appointed to work as ministers to children and families or as youth ministers. Instead, they are considered permissive reporters, which means they are encouraged to report when they have reasonable cause to believe that abuse has occurred. Many state legislatures are reviewing their child abuse reporting statutes and proposing modifications that will add clergy to the list of other specified mandatory reporters. Thus, as your congregation plans this year, it is important to get information on the most up-to-date statutory provisions.

Some states allow reports to be made anonymously, while others do not. If your state allows anonymous reports, it is advisable to take the precaution of making the report by telephone in the presence of an objective witness, such as the church pastor or the church's attorney, who can verify that the report was made (and by whom) in case this is needed later. Many states provide immunity for those making reports of youth and child abuse in good faith.

Notes:

KNOW THE LEGAL REPORTING
requirements for your state.
Get up-to-date information
from your church's attorney or
insurance agent.

This means that the accused cannot bring a lawsuit against the reporter as long as the person had reasonable cause to believe that abuse had occurred.

Every state has statutory definitions of child abuse and child sexual abuse that include abuse of minors up to the age of eighteen. Workers with youth must know these definitions to recognize whether or not the behavior they believe may be abusive meets the statutory definition. A local attorney, or the church's insurance agent, should be consulted to get the current definitions for your state.

Every state's youth and child abuse statutes include a reporting time limit. Once a person becomes aware of or suspects abuse, he or she must report it to the proper authorities within a set amount of time. In some states, this is as short as twenty-four hours. Workers with youth may be subject to criminal penalties, by the requirements of state statutes, for failure to make appropriate and timely reports. Therefore, it is imperative that they be informed of these requirements. Workers must know the correct agencies to which they can report abuse. If state law requires that the local sheriff's department be contacted, the youth group counselor has not made a proper report by simply mentioning her suspicions of abuse to the youth coordinator.

Obviously, it is important to gather accurate information about your state's child abuse statutes before developing the church's reporting procedures. Contact the church's attorney, another local attorney, the local child protective services agency, or your church's insurance agent for help in gathering up-to-date information. Then draft a step-by-step plan for reporting any incident of actual or suspected abuse.

At this point, it will be necessary and important to educate and train all of the church's workers with youth so that they are fully aware of their responsibilities under state law and under the church's prevention policies. Ideally, this education event will include the entire clergy and lay staff of the church; all full-time, part-time, paid, or volunteer workers; all parents of youth; and any others who are interested. Parents need to know that the people caring for their youth at the church are well informed and capable of taking appropriate actions in the event of suspected or alleged abuse. Clergy staff members, even if they are permissive reporters under state law, need to be informed of the law's requirements. **This cannot be overstated: Workers must be fully informed to be able to make lawful reports and to avoid possible criminal penalties for failure to report.**

Beyond the State's Requirements

The church's commitment to the prevention of abuse of youth requires that its workers with youth make reports of abuse according to the requirements of state law. However, our obligations to respond to allegations go beyond the requirements of state law. As Christians, we must also be prepared to respond to others regarding allegations of abuse: the victim and his or her family, the news media, the church's insurance agent, the annual conference, and possibly the abuser.

Faithful response to the victim will include taking the allegation seriously and respecting the victim's privacy, as well as providing sympathetic concern for the victim and his or her family. Faithful response to the victim does not condone blaming the victim or implying that the victim was in any way responsible for causing the abuse.

Faithful response to the annual conference will include notifying conference authorities (the church's district superintendent or the resident bishop) as soon as allegations of abuse are received. Conference authorities must be kept aware of the congregation's actions throughout the process, up to and including the final resolution of the situation. It will also be necessary to notify the church's insurance agent if an allegation of child abuse is made.

Faithful response to the media can be one of the most frightening responsibilities for a local church. However, it can be accomplished fairly simply. In advance, designate one person who will speak to the media. This person may be the pastor, another staff member, the church's attorney, or a lay member of the church, such as the chairperson of the board of trustees. The person chosen must be capable of speaking calmly and thoughtfully in the glare of cameras and microphones. This person must be prepared to answer questions honestly without adding extra or unnecessary information. The designated spokesperson should be given permission to answer questions by saying, "I (we) don't know at this time." **None but the spokesperson should be authorized to speak to the media on behalf of the congregation.**

The designated spokesperson must be prepared to state the church's policy for the prevention of abuse, the church's concern for the safety of the victim and all youth, and the procedures the church has followed to reduce the risk of abuse to youth. Speaking extemporaneously is tempting in situations such as this, but it is ill advised. The designated spokesperson will do well to have a prepared statement, or

Notes:

A COMPREHENSIVE PLAN HAS
—screening and training procedures for workers with youth;
—reporting procedures for allegations of abuse;
—a process for responding to allegations of abuse.

Notes:

THE DESIGNATED SPOKESPERSON must be prepared to state the church's policy for the prevention of abuse, the church's concern for the safety of the victim and all youth, and the procedures the church has followed to reduce the risk of abuse to youth.

at least to have written notes so that the church's policies and procedures can be set forth clearly. The designated spokesperson should never make any statements indicating that the church does not take an allegation seriously or that the church suspects the victim has just made up the story to get attention. The designated spokesperson should not call on members of the youth group to answer questions or to make statements to the media.

Faithful response to the accused abuser will include acknowledgment not only that he or she is a person of sacred worth but also that he or she must stop the abusive behavior, prayerfully repent, and turn in a new direction. Faithful response will include removing the accused from his or her position as a worker with youth until the allegations are fully investigated and resolved. It does not necessarily mean that the accused will at some future time be placed again in a position of trust involving youth. Finally, faithful response does not include forgiving the accused before justice is achieved and the victim is ready to consider whether forgiveness is appropriate or not.

Not If It Happens But When It Happens

Since abuse of youth and children happens every ten seconds and in any location in the United States, it is not so unimaginable that a church could be called on to respond to an allegation of abuse. The local church that has made a commitment to the prevention of abuse in its youth ministry is well on its way to being able to respond faithfully and effectively.

In summary, when an allegation of abuse of any of the youth is made against a worker or member, be prepared to do the following:

- Notify the parents of the victim and take any necessary steps to assure the youth's safety until the parents arrive. The safety of the victim must be the church's primary concern.
- Do not confront the accused abuser with anger and hostility. Treat the accused with dignity, but immediately remove him or her from further involvement with youth.
- Notify the proper law enforcement or child protective services agency.
- Notify the annual conference authorities, the church's insurance agent, and the church's attorney.
- Keep a written record of the steps taken by the church in response to the allegations of abuse.
- Call on your designated spokesperson to make any necessary statements or responses to the news media.

- Prepare a brief and honest statement that can be made to the congregation without giving unnecessary details, placing blame, interfering with the victim's privacy, or violating any confidentiality concerns.
- Be prepared to cooperate fully with the investigation conducted by law enforcement officials or child protective services.

When a local church receives a report or allegation of abuse against a person who has been trusted with the care and nurture of its youth, it is immediately a crisis situation. The best and most faithful response is one that is planned in advance. By careful and thoughtful preparation, the congregation can provide a greater measure of love and concern for the victim and others involved while also cooperating, as necessary, with local authorities. Planning ahead will enable you to preserve your congregation's ability to surround the youth with steadfast love and establish him or her in faith strong enough to withstand any crisis.

Notes:

PLANNING AHEAD WILL

enable you to preserve your congregation's ability to surround the youth with steadfast love and establish him or her in faith strong enough to withstand any crisis.

Notes: _____

_____

_____

_____

_____

_____

_____

_____

_____

_____

_____

Our Response Plan Includes

1.

2.

3.

4.

5.

6.

Our Designated Spokesperson Is _____.

Implementation Strategies for the Congregation

FOR A YOUTH abuse prevention policy to be successful, the wholehearted support of the entire congregation is necessary. Universal support can be developed with a thorough and comprehensive plan for educating the congregation and for including a wide spectrum of members in the development of the policies and procedures.

Give careful consideration to the formation of a committee or task force to prepare the policy. Invite representatives from every group that engages in ministry with youth: Sunday school teachers, fellowship leaders, music ministry leaders, mission event coordinators, and others. Parents and grandparents of middle-high and senior-high grade levels should also be invited, since they can make valuable contributions. By forming an inclusive task force, you will reduce the likelihood of creating policies and procedures that will engender serious opposition from any segments of the congregation. Instead, an inclusive task force will be able to have concerns brought forward and dealt with while the policy is still being developed.

As soon as the task force is formed, it is time to begin working. Start by scheduling a series of at least six meetings. Set your meetings according to the projected completion date of the policy. Many churches have found that six months is a reasonable time frame for their work. Plan for each meeting to last no longer than ninety minutes. The task force will need to accomplish several things, including the following:

- Research issues related to abuse of youth.
- Evaluate the practices of your church related to the care and supervision of youth.
- Develop new policies and procedures for the care and supervision of youth.
- Develop a plan for responding to allegations of abuse of youth.
- Develop a plan for responding to known incidents of abuse of youth.
- Present new policies and procedures to the church council or other approving body.
- Plan to educate the congregation about abuse and the new prevention policies.

FOR THE TASK FORCE TO effectively develop policies and procedures related to abuse of youth, it must have a solid foundation in basic information about abuse.

- Plan to educate the parents of youth about abuse and how to recognize common indicators of abuse.
- Plan to educate the youth about abuse and how to protect themselves.
- Plan training and periodic refresher training about the new policies for all church workers with youth.
- Celebrate!

Task 1:

Research issues related to abuse of youth.

For the task force to effectively develop policies and procedures related to abuse of youth, it must have a solid foundation in basic information about abuse. Without this foundation, creating a prevention policy will be far more difficult. Some of this information could be provided to the task force in writing before the meeting, but plan substantial group discussion time. Steps in completing this task should include the following:

1. Review the definition and types of abuse, using information from pages 15–16.

2. Review the statistics of the frequency of abuse on pages 18–19.

3. Ask the members to think back over the past few weeks and recall incidents of abuse of youth in your community that have been reported in the media.

4. Have the members list the places and settings in which abuse could occur in your congregation, such as Sunday school, youth fellowship, youth choir, other youth-serving groups that meet in the church (Girl Scouts, Boy Scouts, and so forth), and other ministries specific to your congregation.

5. Explore the question, Who are the youth victims of abuse? Youth who are vulnerable as a result of being smaller, weaker, more isolated, more dependent, or more trusting of adults are potential victims. (See pages 23–24 for more information.)

6. Explore the question, Who are the abusers? Abusers cannot be neatly stereotyped. Almost anyone can be an abuser under certain circumstances. No single personality type is likely to become an abuser. No psychological test or tool can accurately predict which person is, or will be, an abuser of youth or children. (See pages 22–23 for more information.) Invite a resource person, such as a parish attorney or a representative of the local

child protective services, to the meeting to present current information about abuse and abusers.

7. Explore the range of frequent reactions from abusers. These include denial, minimization, blame, anger, threats, and manipulation. Task force members, as well as congregational members, need to recognize the typical reactions. When abuse of youth happens and the abuser is confronted, any or all of these reactions may be displayed and may be persuasive.

8. Review the consequences of abuse of youth in the church. A broad range of consequences can be considered: physical injury to the victim, psychological or emotional harm and/or injury to the victim, trauma and distress in the victim's family and the congregation, distress in the abuser's family, and possible legal claims for damages and/or verdicts against the church.

Task 2:
Evaluate the practices of your church related to the care and supervision of youth.

1. Explore the circumstances and situations in the church that could make it easier for an abuser to hurt a youth. These could include inadequate recruiting and screening policies and practices for hiring workers with youth, inadequate supervision of workers, and inadequate control of workers and ministry settings, including a lack of observation and/or evaluation of the workers. Even if your church uses only volunteer workers with youth, the workers must be adequately supervised and evaluated to assure that ministry is being accomplished safely. When the task force members have identified the circumstances that make abuse possible, they will be better able to understand and identify the ways that abuse can be prevented. Then the task force can move on to developing and integrating a comprehensive prevention policy. The "Local Church Self-Evaluation Form" (page 89) will be a useful instrument here.

2. Identify current policies. Even if there is no written policy, your church is undoubtedly operating under a set of unwritten rules that the members understand to be the way things are done. For instance, if your church has no written policy regarding the supervision of youth on a summer mission trip, there is quite likely an understanding among the parents, youth, and workers about who can serve as chaperones for the trip and how many will be needed. The task force needs to identify the current practices of the church, whether

Notes:

EVERY CONGREGATION IS
capable of assuring that its church building is a place of security and peace for its youth.

Notes:

written or unwritten, and decide which are adequate, inadequate, and/or in need of modification.

3. Review the current policies regarding the recruiting and screening of workers with youth (including paid workers and volunteers, lay and clergy staff members). Review the policies related to training workers regarding abuse and how to report allegations and/or incidents. Review the policies for supervising workers with youth. Review the current practices of how youth are disciplined to determine whether the methods used are appropriate. Be sure that corporal punishment is excluded. Review the facilities used for ministries with youth to determine whether they are suitable and safe. For instance, are the facilities too isolated from the rest of the church? Youth areas are often isolated from the rest of the church building or property. If this is your situation, consider possible alternative locations. These facilities should not be isolated but should provide openness and visibility for the participants and for the parents coming to pick up their youth.

Task 3:
Develop new policies and procedures for the care and supervision of youth.
At this point, the group will begin to integrate what it has learned about abuse and the current circumstances in the congregation. The following practical components need to be considered:
- recruiting and screening practices;
- applications;
- references;
- disclosure forms;
- background checks/consent forms;
- covenant statements;
- use of appropriate facilities for ministries with youth;
- appropriate types of discipline for youth.

The sample forms on pages 76–92 will be helpful as the task force develops recruiting and screening forms tailored to the specific circumstances of your congregation. It is important to identify which group in the church will be responsible for the periodic review and updating of the policies and procedures, since the task force will probably not be an ongoing group.

Task 4:
Develop a plan for responding to allegations of abuse of youth.
Even though the task force has drafted youth abuse prevention policies and procedures related to recruiting, screening,

REVIEW THE FACILITIES USED
for ministries with youth to determine whether they are suitable and safe.

and hiring workers, it must also draft a detailed and comprehensive plan for responding to allegations of abuse, if and when they occur. The primary goal must always be to protect the victim from further harm and to protect the victim's privacy.

Furthermore, any plan designed for your congregation must comply with the laws of your state and local jurisdiction. Although this resource provides helpful ideas, it does not substitute for a consultation with your parish attorney or a local attorney familiar with the current requirements for reporting allegations of abuse in your state. It would be appropriate to invite a resource person to meet with the task force or to request a written copy of the state laws about child abuse reporting requirements. Possible resource people are attorneys from the district attorney's staff, school counselors, and staff members from the Department of Family and Children's Services.

Your response plan should designate a person (or more than one) who will receive reports of abuse and follow through on them, according to the requirements of your state law. This can be a clergy staff person, a lay staff member, or someone else who is trusted. However, it must be someone who will honor the confidentiality of the reports. When a report or an allegation of abuse is received, this person must be prepared to follow the response plan. He or she needs to remember that youth generally do not lie about abuse. However, the designated person also needs to be aware that false allegations can be made, especially in circumstances involving custody battles. Knowledge about abuse and familiarity with the youth and families of the congregation are important resources for the person receiving the reports of abuse.

Your plan should also designate a person who will be responsible for any necessary communication with the media (pages 53–54). This does not have to be the senior pastor. It can be any person who is capable of answering questions under pressure. Take care to designate only one person for this responsibility.

Your response plan must include keeping adequate documentation of any allegations of abuse. Have incident report forms readily available. A sample form is on pages 86–87. The information on the form must be kept confidential and limited to only those who must know, such as the legal authorities specified by your state law, the pastor, the district superintendent, the bishop, the church's insurance agent, the parish attorney, and possibly the chair of the staff-parish relations committee. Plan carefully who will have access to

Notes:

POSSIBLE RESOURCE PEOPLE
are attorneys from the district attorney's staff, school counselors, and staff members from the Department of Family and Children's Services.

Notes:

EXPERIENCE HAS SHOWN THAT inadequate response plans do not do enough to assist the victim, making it infinitely more difficult for the victim and the congregation to experience spiritual healing.

the forms and where the forms will be stored. It is advisable to keep records in a locked file. Emphasize the necessity of documenting all actions and conversations related to allegations of abuse.

Task 5:
Develop a plan for responding to known incidents of abuse of youth.
These steps will be similar to those for responding to allegations of abuse; however, several additional components are necessary. Appropriate response to a known incident must include a plan for providing emergency care for the victim, a plan for notifying parents as well as legal authorities, a plan for protecting evidence, a plan for communicating with the media, a process for documenting every action taken and every report made, a plan for removing the abuser from any further contact with youth, a plan for enlisting the full cooperation of the church staff, and a plan providing for pastoral care to the victim and his or her family. Your congregation may also wish to include a plan for providing pastoral care for the family of the abuser. In some situations, this may be more appropriately handled through a minister from a nearby church. Experience has shown over the past few years that thorough response plans are crucial in helping the victim cope with his or her injury and begin healing physically and spiritually. Experience has also shown that inadequate response plans do not do enough to assist the victim, making it infinitely more difficult for the victim and the congregation to experience spiritual healing. Although litigation is not a healing or therapeutic process, some survivors of abuse pursue litigation when they think the church's response inadequately acknowledges their injuries.

Task 6:
Present new policies and procedures to the church council or other approving body.
When the task force has drafted the policies and procedures outlined above, it will be ready to present its work to the church council or other approving body for endorsement and adoption. Ideally, the task force will have made regular progress reports and given the church council educational information regarding all of the issues related to prevention of abuse of youth.

Task 7:
Plan to educate the congregation about abuse and the new prevention policies.
This will need to be a shared responsibility of the task force and the church council. Educating the membership about abuse and the new policies cannot be accomplished in one

meeting of the church council, in one letter to parents, or in one article in the church newsletter. While developing these policies, the task force members will come to understand how difficult it is to comprehend the possibility that sexual abuse of youth could occur in the church. Comprehension of the harm caused by abuse does not come through one committee meeting. Similarly, full understanding as to how abuse can be prevented also takes time. The church council and the task force will be far more successful in achieving substantial support among the congregation's membership if they work together to inform the congregation, over time, about pertinent issues and plans being developed for prevention. Remember that people are more apt to respond to information that is presented in a variety of ways. Educate the membership by using a combination of parent meetings, Sunday school classes, youth fellowship orientation and training meetings, newsletter articles, church bulletin inserts, video presentations, spoken words from the pulpit during worship, and letters from the task force.

Task 8:
Plan training and periodic refresher training about the new policies for all church workers with youth.
An initial orientation and training of all workers with youth should include information about the nature of abuse and its consequences for youth, ways to prevent abuse, and ways to respond to abuse. The training should also educate the workers about the church's new abuse prevention policies and the plan for implementing the policies. A suggested training plan is provided in Chapter 8. Finally, the task force and the church council will need to designate a group in the church that will be responsible for providing ongoing training and orientation during the year for new workers with youth.

Task 9:
Celebrate!
A brief review of this chapter makes it plain that the implementation of a youth sexual abuse prevention plan in your congregation will not be accomplished with one brief meeting and vote. Those who accept the invitation to serve on the task force and develop the abuse prevention plan will be making a sizable commitment of time and energy. When their work is complete and your congregation has adopted a plan, the church should have a great celebration.

Plan a time of commitment and rejoicing for the Sunday morning worship services. Use special music, banners, leaders, and plenty of youth to create the worship celebration. Give special recognition to the task force members, and

Notes:

COMPREHENSION OF THE HARM caused by abuse does not come through one committee meeting.

Notes:

_____

_____

_____

_____

_____

_____

_____

_____

_____

_____

_____

_____

_____

express the congregation's gratitude for the work they have done. Focus the worship celebration on the congregational commitment to make your church a sacred and safe place in which all can encounter the love and saving grace of our Lord, Jesus Christ. A suggested order of worship is found on pages 93–94.

WHEN YOUR CONGREGATION

has adopted a plan, the church should have a great celebration.

chapter eight

A Model for Training Workers

IMPLEMENTING a comprehensive strategy for the prevention of youth abuse in a local church cannot be done without a substantial amount of education being provided for the workers with youth, the parents of youth, the congregation, and the youth themselves. This model is designed to be used with your church's workers with youth, but you may easily modify it for use with other groups. This model is designed to be used as a three- or a four-hour workshop.

I. Opening Worship

A. Prayer of Invocation

Gracious and most merciful God, you have brought us together in witness to your love of all youth and children. Open our hearts and minds now, and prepare us to receive your wisdom. Show us your will and fill us with courage to face the reality of abuse of youth in our community. Give us energy and dedication enough to make this, your church, a holy and hallowed place where all your youth may be safe and secure as they grow in faith and in their knowledge of your presence in their lives. Amen.

B. Suggested Scriptures
1. Jeremiah 1:4-19
2. Micah 6:6-8
3. Luke 2:21-24 and 40-52
4. 1 Corinthians 13:4-8

C. Brief Devotion

You may begin by recalling the confirmation ritual for youth, reminding the participants of the pledge made by the congregation at each youth's confirmation. Acknowledge and list the many ways your congregation lives out that pledge through its current ministries with youth. Conclude by introducing the youth abuse prevention strategy as the newest component of your church's ministries with youth.

Notes:

EDUCATION AND TRAINING
are essential for the successful implementation of policies and procedures to reduce the risk of abuse.

II. Introductory Information

A. Current Occurrences

Set the stage here for the substance of the event by introducing recent news reports from your own community's newspapers or television broadcasts related to incidents of abuse of youth in any locations and institutions. In this section, present the material related to any current litigation involving the church and claims of abuse of youth. You can make this a small-group activity by bringing a variety of newspapers, magazines, and other sources for the participants to review. Have them pull out the reports of abuse and any resulting litigation and then tell the whole group their findings.

B. Current Statistics

Quote the statistical information from this resource or from other sources available to you. Work the math on a chalkboard or newsprint to show how three million annual incidents finally translate into one incident of abuse every ten seconds (pages 18–19).

C. Reasons to Implement a Youth Abuse Prevention Strategy
1. Our church is a community of faith that can offer a safe haven and sanctuary where youth can seek advice, help, and nurture.
2. Our church is a place where more than just facts of abuse can be taught. We can also teach and proclaim our Christian values: compassion, justice, repentance, and grace.
3. Our church is a place where youth can come to learn and develop the inner strength and spiritual resources they will need to feel truly connected to God and to face suffering and evil.
4. Our church can be a place where youth and adults are able to learn how to respond to painful and confusing events using the wisdom of the Scriptures.

D. Summarize

These reports and data demonstrate that we cannot ignore the possibility that abuse could happen here. For the sake of our youth and the protection of our workers against false allegations, we need to intentionally work to prevent abuse.

III. What Is Abuse and How Can We Recognize It?

Use the information on pages 15–16 and 21–22 to give definitions and indicators of abuse.

A. Physical abuse
B. Emotional abuse
C. Neglect
D. Sexual abuse
E. Ritual abuse

IV. Who Are Abusers?: The Balance of Power

Use the information and examples provided on pages 22–23. Discuss the concepts of power and vulnerability and how these can lead to abuse. Use the news reports you shared earlier to help demonstrate the balance-of-power concept. In each account, have the participants list the sources of power available to the abuser. Then have the participants identify the factors that made the youth victim vulnerable to the abuser.

If time allows, you may use a video to illustrate the concepts you have just addressed. The resource list (pages 95–96) provides suggestions of appropriate videos or sources for videos.

V. What Are We Doing to Keep Our Youth and Workers Safe?

Present the new policies and procedures for the prevention of youth abuse. Give participants time to read the policies. Allow time for questions and discussion as you review each section with the group.

A. Screening of Staff (Employees and Volunteers)
    Use your policies and the information in this resource for the substance of this section. Provide copies of all screening forms, application forms, covenant forms, consent forms, and position description forms. Allow time for a review of each form and for questions from the participants.

B. Training of Staff (Employees and Volunteers)
    Use your policies and the information in this resource for the substance of this section. Be thorough in reviewing all of the safety procedures, and allow time for questions.

C. Reporting Suspected Abuse
    Use your policies and the information in this resource to explain the reporting procedure developed for your church. Explain the policy, the procedure for making a report, and the concept of confidentiality.

Notes:

HELP WORKERS WITH YOUTH understand that the policies are to protect the workers as well as the youth.

Notes:

D. Completing the Task
If this is the first occasion the workers have had to see and review the screening, application, and position description forms, you may need to allow time for each of them to complete the forms.

VI. Closing Worship

A. Covenant Forms
Have one or two people distribute covenant forms to the participants. Say, "We have reached the end of our time together today. Let's prepare to celebrate our church's commitment to protecting our children, youth, and those who work with them. Please read the covenant you have just received, and sign it as your commitment to our church's ministry with children and youth."

B. Return to the Scripture Reading From the Opening Worship. Read aloud the verses from 1 Corinthians 13:4-8.

C. Invite the participants to pray responsively by saying, after each sentence prayer, "We welcome the youth!"

Leader:	O God, by our presence here today,
People:	**We welcome the youth!**
Leader:	O God, by our promises in confirmation,
People:	**We welcome the youth!**
Leader:	O God, by our participation in the ministries of this congregation,
People:	**We welcome the youth!**
Leader:	O God, by our commitment to keeping this place holy and safe in every way,
People:	**We welcome the youth!**
Leader:	O God, give us wisdom, strength, and courage enough to show the world that
People:	**We welcome the youth!**
ALL:	**Amen!**

D. Offering
Ask the participants to bring forward their signed covenant forms as a sign of offering themselves in ministry with children and youth. Sing the Doxology.

E. Benediction
May the grace of the Lord Jesus Christ, the love of God, and the power of the Holy Spirit guide and direct you in all you do. Amen.

WELCOME THE YOUTH
by offering yourselves in ministry to youth.

After Abuse, Then What?

chapter nine

WHEN THE ABUSE of a youth occurs in the church, there are many victims in addition to the one who has been physically harmed; and all are in need of healing ministry. Who are the other victims?

The other victims may include
- family members of the teen who was harmed;
- peers of the youth;
- parents of the youth victim's peers;
- remaining workers with youth;
- congregation as a community of faith;
- family of the accused abuser.

Each victim will need to be included in a ministry of comfort and healing, but the needs of each victim may be somewhat different from the others.

Abuse of youth and children, either within the church or outside of the church, is not a new phenomenon. It has existed for longer than we can remember. What is a relatively new phenomenon is our recognition that the harm of abuse is exponentially magnified when it occurs within the church and is kept secret. Abuse that is hidden continues to cause anger, confusion, and fear in the congregation for years to come. I know of a congregation in which a teenager was abused by an adult worker with youth more than two decades ago, and to this day the real truth of what happened has not been shared with the whole congregation. The congregation has suffered from feelings of anger and fear for years, with a result that no pastor has been able to serve there more than two years. It has become a singularly depressing appointment to serve. The failure to address the issues of anger, fear, and grief that occurred within the church after the incident of abuse have had far-reaching and devastating consequences for everyone.

How can your church be in ministry to all, or any, of the victims of abuse? After abuse is experienced, the ministry of recovery must be aimed at assuring justice for all and healing for those who are suffering. Justice and healing will not be achieved in a short time. Your congregation may need to spend a year

Notes:

FAILURE TO ADDRESS THE issues of anger, fear, and grief that occur within the church after abuse can have far-reaching and devastating consequences.

or more working toward healing and justice. Simply sponsoring a workshop, showing a video, or preaching a sermon will not create the measure of understanding needed for healing and justice to be achieved. The ministry with victims of abuse, both the individual and the congregation, can be likened to ministry with those in grief. Thinking in these terms, you will begin to grasp the length of time needed for the victims and congregation as a whole to be restored to a feeling of health and justice.

The First Step

The first step in ministry with victims of abuse in a congregation must be truth telling, an honest communication about what has happened. Truth telling does not mean engaging in gossip or speculation. Above all, remember that truth telling never means blaming the youth victim in any way.

How will you engage in honest communication? Follow the procedures you have already planned for reporting an incident of abuse to law enforcement authorities and denominational officials. By the time you have done that, rumors will have begun to spread among the members of the congregation. At this point, it is important to provide honest and forthright information. This may begin with a letter to the members that briefly explains the incident and the initial action taken by the church. Such a letter should not include the identification of the youth victim or that of the accused abuser. On the other hand, it should include a statement of the actions taken to assure the safety of all the youth and to assure your congregation's continuing ability to provide ministry to youth. The letter should put to rest rumors and innuendo and assure everyone that everything possible has been done to provide for the safety of the victim and to enable the safe continuation of the church's ministry.

The Congregational Meeting

A congregational meeting can be a powerful aspect of the ministry of truth telling. However, if thoughtful and prayerful preparation for such a meeting is not done, it can become an occasion of anger and confusion. Therefore, schedule a meeting for a specific time and place, and make plans for it. Do not simply say during announcements in the Sunday morning worship service, "As you may have heard, an allegation of abuse on one of our youth has been made, and now is just as good a time as any to discuss what happened." An impromptu invitation can, and probably will, be more harmful than helpful. It may force members to participate in a discussion they would prefer to avoid. It may shock members who have not heard reports or rumors. It may cause some to suddenly remember previous trauma in their lives and evoke severe emotional reactions. This approach may also insult the family of the youth victim by making it appear that the abuse in your church is nothing more than an item on the list of Sunday morning announcements. The consequences of such a cavalier approach, in subsequent litigation, could be harmful for the church.

Planning carefully for a congregational meeting is crucial. Give everyone notice so that they may choose whether to attend. Specifically select the leaders for the meeting. In most cases, it will be important for the pastor to be a leader. However, if the pastor is the accused abuser, he or she cannot lead the meeting. Also, in most cases, it is important to have present lay leaders and representatives from the annual conference (such as the district superintendent). The lay leaders will be able to provide information about the actions taken by the church. The district superintendent may not need to do anything more than reinforce the support of the annual conference as the congregation deals with this crisis. Even so, this is a valuable contribution and should not be overlooked. Finally, the leadership team for the congregational meeting should include a qualified counselor who is not necessarily a member of the congregation. The counselor can immediately help those who experience strong feelings. If your annual conference has a Response Team, invite them to the meeting. This team is a small group of people trained to come to your church and guide the victims, both the individual and the congregation, through a healthy and compassionate response process. Their insight, experience, and wisdom will be invaluable.

Meeting Agenda

What should happen in a congregational meeting following an incident of abuse of youth? Include these elements:
- fact sharing;
- small-group sharing time;
- closing moments of reflection and worship.

Open the fact sharing by giving an accurate description of what happened and what actions have been taken, or will be taken. Answer questions as accurately as possible without jeopardizing any ongoing investigation by the church or local law enforcement agencies. Protect the identity of the victim, especially if the family has requested privacy. Do not be afraid to answer, "We don't know the answer to that yet." It is far better to admit not knowing the answer than

Notes:

A CAREFULLY PLANNED congregational meeting can be a powerful aspect of the ministry of truth telling.

Notes:

IT IS FAR BETTER TO ADMIT not knowing the answer than to speculate about the incident or outcome.

to speculate about the incident or outcome. Your annual conference Response Team can guide you in how to provide information and protect privacy for the victim.

The small-group sharing time could be the most important segment of the meeting. Divide the participants into groups of five or six. Have a facilitator for each group. If your conference has a Response Team, the team members are trained to serve as facilitators. If there is not a Response Team, your annual conference may be able to suggest facilitators in your area. The facilitator will begin by saying that it is permissible to express any feeling or emotion within the small group. All will be allowed time to speak, and there will be no debate about the feelings or emotions expressed. The purpose of this segment of the meeting is to help people identify and verbalize their feelings about the incident, not to strategize a response or elicit premature forgiveness toward the abuser. This part of the meeting may take an hour or more.

When it is apparent that the small groups are able to bring their time together to a close, reassemble the whole group. Acknowledge the reality of this painful situation, and offer a prayer for the congregation as it seeks to achieve justice for all involved and healing for all who are suffering.

Continuing Ministry

The initial actions of the church are only the first steps in what may be a long process of restoring the victim and the congregation to spiritual health. One letter or one congregational meeting probably will not be all your church needs. Based on the feelings, fears, and needs expressed in the congregational meeting, you can develop a plan for continuing ministry. It may be useful to appoint a task force for this planning process, just as you used a task force to develop the youth abuse prevention policies and procedures. Another approach is to use existing groups within the church to plan appropriate ministries of healing, justice, education, and worship. The annual conference Response Team can provide valuable insight and expertise as you plan for continuing healing ministries.

As the group begins its work, it will be well advised to consider several types of ministry: educational, supportive, and any others that have been suggested by group members.

Educational ministries may include programs on
- the consequences of abuse of youth;
- how to comfort families suffering from abuse;
- how youth can protect themselves from abuse;

- resources in your community for victims/survivors;
- other topics of concern.

Programs may include adult survivors of abuse who are able to tell how they achieved healing and recovery. Programs like these can be carried out through Sunday school classes, youth groups, or other settings. It is important to remember that none of these programs should be provided without advance notice and publicity. In this way, you ensure that those who wish to participate can make their plans and that those who do not wish to participate can avoid being involved.

Support ministries can be developed within your congregation for families suffering as a result of abuse, as well as for youth victims of abuse. Identify qualified leaders within your congregation or community, and enlist their aid in organizing support groups. Your conference Response Team may be able to train support group leaders. Providing individual counseling for the victim, the victim's family, and other affected members of the congregation can also be an important ministry. Your congregation may be able to make the necessary financial arrangements with a trained and experienced counselor so that the victim and/or his or her family can receive sufficient counseling to achieve healing. This type of ministry may also be important to the family members of the accused abuser. While it would be inappropriate to condone in any way the behavior of the abuser, it is appropriate to recognize that the family of the abuser may suffer terribly. Thus, offering counseling to them may be an act of grace and healing without condoning the abusive behavior. Your local community is likely to have a variety of resources available that would be useful in developing such counseling and support groups. For instance, leaders may be available through other congregations or support groups that already exist.

Programming with youth that is aimed at restoring their trust in the church and in its workers will be a valuable support ministry. Programs and discussion groups that focus on justice, mercy, and reconciliation in difficult situations will set a solid foundation for their continuing spiritual growth. Programming of this nature will require extensive planning and qualified leadership. No matter how much work is required, it is worth it if just one youth is enabled to feel safe in the church again. We must not underestimate the importance of this aspect of healing after abuse. Youth who are aware that abuse occurs will need lots of opportunities to talk, ask questions, and think for themselves about how the tragedy happened and how they can protect themselves and one another from future problems. If the adults in the

Notes:

_____

_____

_____

_____

_____

_____

_____

_____

_____

_____

_____

_____

BASED ON THE FEELINGS, fears, and needs expressed in the congregational meeting, you can develop a plan for continuing ministry.

Notes:

THE MORE A CONGREGATION
does to encourage openness
and honesty in communication,
the faster healing and recovery
can proceed.

congregation fail to be open to questions and refuse to help the youth think about how to restore trust, the adults will have failed to increase their faith and confirm their hope.

These ideas and plans for continuing ministries are based on the concept that the more your congregation does to encourage openness and honesty in communication, the faster healing and recovery can proceed for everyone. No matter how long the process takes, there are two things that should never be allowed: blaming the victim and offering forgiveness to the abuser without any sign of repentance from the abuser. The youth who is abused is never responsible for being abused and did not do anything to cause it. Therefore, do not let your church attempt to assuage its conscience with words like, "Well, we did all we could to prevent something like this, but she asked for it!" This kind of remark does not foster open and honest communication. Instead, it blames the victim, denies the truth, and insults the victim and the victim's family.

Offering gratuitous forgiveness to the abuser is of no benefit in the healing process for the victim or for the congregation. For healing to occur, painful consequences must be endured not just by the victim, who suffers first, but also by the abuser. When the abuser is truly able to live a changed life and demonstrate sorrow and repentance, then it will it be possible for the congregation to offer the grace of forgiveness. Even so, the victim may or may not be able to forgive the harm he or she has suffered, and no pressure to forgive should ever be brought to bear on the victim simply to help the abuser feel better.

After enough time has passed, your response group may want to organize a time for sharing that is similar to that in the first congregational meeting. Such a meeting can be used to assess how much healing and recovery has occurred. Identify any remaining needs or issues that have not been resolved and possible ways to address them. The natural tendency in individuals, and in congregations, is to hide or try to ignore the pain, which creates the need for regular follow-up.

Finally, your response group will perhaps want to plan a worship celebration to express gratitude for the progress that has been made toward healing and recovery and to express joy in the congregation's united efforts to do justice and to trust in the abiding grace and love of Jesus Christ, our Savior. Your annual conference Response Team can be helpful in planning such a service of healing.

Sample Forms

PLEASE NOTE THAT all of the forms, checklists, and other items in this section are samples and need to be modified to meet your specific needs. Permission is given to reproduce these forms for churches who have purchased *Safe Sanctuaries for Youth: Reducing the Risk of Abuse in Youth Ministries.*

Items include

1. Membership Form for the Local Church Task Force for the Prevention of Abuse of Youth in the Church

2. Youth Abuse Prevention Policy

3. Employment Application

4. Authorization and Request for Criminal Records Check

5. Volunteer Application

6. Form for Reference Check

7. Participation Covenant for All Workers With Youth

8. Report of Suspected Incident of Youth Abuse

9. Accident Report Form

10. Local Church Self-Evaluation Form

11. Youth Ministry Staff Worker Position Description

12. Director of Youth Ministry/Minister for Youth Position Description

13. Order of Worship: A Celebration of Our Commitment to Youth

MEMBERSHIP FORM FOR THE LOCAL CHURCH TASK FORCE
FOR THE PREVENTION OF ABUSE OF YOUTH IN THE CHURCH

Pastor
Name: _____
Address: _____
Phone: _____

Member of Staff-Parish Committee
Name: _____
Address: _____
Phone: _____

Member of Board of Trustees
Name: _____
Address: _____
Phone: _____

Lay Leader
Name: _____
Address: _____
Phone: _____

Minister of Youth/Director of Youth Ministries
Name: _____
Address: _____
Phone: _____

Representative From Each Group Working With Youth
(These groups may include Sunday school, youth fellowship groups, youth choir, and others. The number of members listed here will depend on the number of groups active in your congregation.)
Name: _____
Address: _____
Phone: _____

Name: _____
Address: _____
Phone: _____

Name: _____
Address: _____
Phone: _____

Representative From Parents of Youth
(The number of parent representatives will vary based on the size of your youth group. Having at least two parents, from separate families, is the recommended minimum number.)
Name: _____
Address: _____
Phone: _____

Name: _____
Address: _____
Phone: _____

YOUTH ABUSE PREVENTION POLICY

Introduction

The General Conference of The United Methodist Church, in April 1996, adopted a resolution aimed at reducing the risk of sexual abuse of youth and children in the church. The adopted resolution includes the following statement:

Jesus said, "Whoever welcomes [a] child...welcomes me" (Matthew 18:5). Children are our present and our future, our hope, our teachers, our inspiration. They are full participants in the life of the church and in the realm of God.

Jesus also said, "If any of you put a stumbling block before one of these little ones…, it would be better for you if a great millstone were fastened around your neck and you were drowned in the depth of the sea" (Matthew 18:6). Our Christian faith calls us to offer both hospitality and protection to the little ones, the children. The Social Principles of The United Methodist Church state that "children must be protected from economic, physical, emotional, and sexual exploitation and abuse" (¶ 162C).

Tragically, churches have not always been safe places for children. Child sexual abuse, exploitation, and ritual abuse ("ritual abuse" refers to abusive acts committed as part of ceremonies or rites; ritual abusers are often related to cults, or pretend to be) occur in churches, both large and small, urban and rural. The problem cuts across all economic, cultural, and racial lines. It is real, and it appears to be increasing. Most annual conferences can cite specific incidents of child sexual abuse and exploitation within churches. Virtually every congregation has among its members adult survivors of early sexual trauma.

Such incidents are devastating to all who are involved: the child, the family, the local church and its leaders. Increasingly, churches are torn apart by the legal, emotional, and monetary consequences of litigation following allegations of abuse.

God calls us to make our churches safe places, protecting children and other vulnerable persons from sexual and ritual abuse. God calls us to create communities of faith where children and adults grow safe and strong.

(From *The Book of Resolutions of The United Methodist Church—2000; pages 180–81.*
Copyright © 2000 by The United Methodist Publishing House. Used by permission.)

Thus, in covenant with all United Methodist congregations, we adopt this policy for the prevention of abuse of youth in our church.

Purpose

Our congregation's purpose for establishing this Youth Abuse Prevention Policy and accompanying procedures is to demonstrate our absolute and unwavering commitment to the physical safety and spiritual growth of all our youth.

Statement of Covenant

Therefore, as a Christian community of faith and a United Methodist congregation, we pledge to conduct the ministry of the gospel in ways that assure the safety and spiritual growth of all our children and youth as well as all of the workers with children and youth. We will follow reasonable safety measures in the selection and recruitment of workers; we will implement prudent operational procedures in all programs and events; we will educate all our workers with children and youth regarding the use of all appropriate policies and methods (including first aid and methods of discipline); we will have a clearly defined procedure for reporting a suspected incident of abuse that conforms to the requirements of state law; and we will be prepared to respond to media inquiries if an incident occurs.

Conclusion

In all of our ministries with youth, this congregation is committed to demonstrating the love of Jesus Christ so that each youth will be "surrounded by steadfast love,...established in the faith, and confirmed and strengthened in the way that leads to life eternal" (From "Congregational Pledge 2," "Baptismal Covenant II," in *The United Methodist Hymnal*, page 44).

EMPLOYMENT APPLICATION

(This type of application should be completed by all who seek any position that will involve the supervision and/or custody of youth. You should tailor the application to the specific circumstances in your congregation. However, the employment application should include, at a minimum, sections for personal identification, job qualifications, experience and background, references, and a waiver/consent to a criminal records check.)

Name: _____
          Last   First   Middle

Are you over the age of 18?   ☐ Yes   ☐ No

Present address: _____

City: _____ State: _____ Zip: _____

Home phone: _____

Position applied for: _____

Date you are available to start: _____

Qualifications:

Academic achievements: (Schools attended, degrees earned, dates of completion)

_____

_____

_____

Continuing education completed: (Courses taken, dates of completion)

_____

_____

_____

Professional organizations: (List any in which you have membership)

_____

_____

_____

First aid training? ☐ Yes ☐ No   Date completed: _____

CPR training?   ☐ Yes ☐ No   Date completed: _____

Previous Work Experience: Please list your previous employers from the past five years. Include the job title, a description of position duties and responsibilities, the name of the company/employer, the address of the company/employer, the name of your immediate supervisor, and the dates you were employed in each position.

_____

_____

_____

_____

_____

_____

_____

Previous Volunteer Experience: Please list any relevant volunteer positions you have held. List the duties you performed in each position, the name of your supervisor, the address and phone number of the volunteer organization, and the dates of your volunteer service.

_____

_____

_____

_____

_____

_____

_____

Have you ever been convicted of or pled guilty to a crime, either a misdemeanor or a felony (including but not limited to drug-related charges, child abuse, other crimes of violence, theft, or motor vehicle violations)?   ☐ No   ☐ Yes

If yes, please explain:

_____

_____

References: Please list as references three individuals who are not related to you by blood or marriage. List people who have known you for at least three years.

1. Name: _____
   Address: _____
   Daytime Phone: _____
   Evening Phone: _____
   Length of time you have known reference: _____
   Relationship to reference: _____

2. Name: _____
   Address: _____
   Daytime Phone: _____
   Evening Phone: _____
   Length of time you have known reference: _____
   Relationship to reference: _____

3. Name: _____
   Address: _____
   Daytime Phone: _____
   Evening Phone: _____
   Length of time you have known reference: _____
   Relationship to reference: _____

Waiver and Consent:

I, _____, hereby certify that the information I have provided on this application for employment is true and correct. I authorize this church to verify the information I have provided on this application by contacting the references and employers I have listed, by conducting a criminal records check, or by other means, including contacting others whom I have not listed. I authorize the references and employers listed in this application to give you whatever information they may have regarding my character and fitness for the job for which I have applied. Furthermore, I waive any rights I may have to confidentiality.

In the event that my application is accepted and I become employed by _____ Church, I agree to abide by and be bound by the policies of _____ Church and to refrain from inappropriate conduct in the performance of my duties on behalf of _____ Church.

I have read this waiver and the entire application, and I am fully aware of its contents. I sign this consent freely and under no duress or coercion.

_____   _____
Signature of Applicant   Date

_____   _____
Witness   Date

This is a sample form. Please tailor your congregation's form to comply with the reporting requirements of the laws of your state and your congregation's policies.

AUTHORIZATION AND REQUEST FOR CRIMINAL RECORDS CHECK

I, _____ , hereby authorize _____ Church to request the _____ police/sheriff's department, or another company, to release information regarding any record of charges or convictions contained in its files, or in any criminal file maintained on me, whether said file is a local, state, or national file, and including but not limited to accusations and convictions for crimes committed against minors, to the fullest extent permitted by state and federal law. I do release said police/sheriff's department, or other company, from all liability that may result from any such disclosure made in response to this request.

_____

Signature of Applicant   Date

Print applicant's full name: _____

Print all other names that have been used by applicant (if any):

_____

Date of birth: _____ Place of birth: _____

Social Security number: _____

Driver's license number: _____ State issuing license: _____

License expiration date: _____

Request sent to: _____

    Name: _____

    Address: _____

    Phone: _____

List each address at which you have resided in the last five years.

    Address: _____

    Address: _____

    Address: _____

Applicant's Current Name: _____

    Address: _____

    Phone: _____

This is a sample form. Your local police or sheriff's department may have its own request form and prefer that you use it.

VOLUNTEER APPLICATION

Name: _____

Address: _____

Daytime phone: _____ Evening phone: _____

Occupation: _____

Employer: _____

Current job responsibilities and schedule: _____

_____

Previous work experience: _____

Previous volunteer experience: _____

_____

Special interests, hobbies, and skills: _____

How many hours per week are you available to volunteer? _____

_____ Days _____ Evenings _____ Weekends

Can you make a one-year commitment to this volunteer role? _____

Do you have your own transportation? _____

Do you have a valid driver's license? _____

Do you have liability insurance? (List policy limits and name of carrier) _____

Why would you like to volunteer as a worker with youth?

_____

_____

What qualities do you have that would help you work with youth?

_____

_____

How were you parented as a child? _____

_____

If you are the parent of teenagers, how do you discipline them? _____

Have you ever been charged with, convicted of, or pled guilty to a crime, either a misdemeanor or a felony (including but not limited to drug-related charges, child abuse, other crimes of violence, theft, or motor vehicle violations)? ☐ No ☐ Yes
If yes, please explain fully:

_____

_____

Have you ever been exposed to an incident of abuse of a teenager? ☐ No ☐ Yes
If yes, how did you feel about the incident? _____

Would you be available for periodic volunteer training sessions? ☐ Yes ☐ No

References: Please list three personal references (people who are not related to you by blood or marriage) and provide complete address and phone information for each. References are confidential.

1. Name: _____

   Address: _____

   Daytime phone: _____

   Evening phone: _____

   Relationship to reference: _____

2. Name: _____

   Address: _____

   Daytime phone: _____

   Evening phone: _____

   Relationship to reference: _____

3. Name: _____

   Address: _____

   Daytime phone: _____

   Evening phone: _____

   Relationship to reference: _____

_____
Signature of Applicant   Date

This is a sample form. Use it as a guide for tailoring your own application based on your congregation's needs.

FORM FOR REFERENCE CHECK

Applicant name: _____

Reference name: _____

Reference address: _____

Reference phone: _____

1. What is your relationship to the applicant?

2. How long have you known the applicant?

3. How well do you know the applicant?

4. How would you describe the applicant?

5. How would you describe the applicant's ability to relate to youth?

6. How would you describe the applicant's ability to relate to adults?

7. How would you describe the applicant's leadership abilities?

8. Would you describe the applicant as someone who prefers team sports or individual competitions?

9. How would you feel about having the applicant as a volunteer worker with your youth?

10. Do you know of any characteristics that would negatively affect the applicant's ability to work with youth? If so, please describe them.

11. Do you have any knowledge that the applicant has ever been convicted of a crime? If so, please describe.

12. Please list any other comments you would like to make:

Reference inquiry completed by: _____
                                          Signature   Date

This is a sample form. Please tailor it to the specific needs of your local congregation. A form like this can also be used to conduct a telephone interview with the reference.

PARTICIPATION COVENANT FOR ALL WORKERS WITH YOUTH

The congregation of _____ Church is committed to providing a safe and secure environment for all youth and volunteers who participate in ministries and activities sponsored by the church. The following policy statements reflect our congregation's commitment to preserving this church as a holy place of safety and protection for all who would enter and as a place in which all people can experience the love of God through relationships with others.

1. No adult who has been convicted of child abuse (either sexual, physical, or emotional) should volunteer to work with children or youth in any church-sponsored activity.
2. Adult survivors of child abuse need the love and support of our congregation. Any adult survivor who desires to volunteer in some capacity to work with youth is encouraged to discuss his/her willingness with one of our church's ministers before accepting an assignment.
3. All adult volunteers involved with the youth of our church must have been members of the congregation for at least six months before beginning a volunteer assignment.
4. Adult volunteers with youth shall observe the two-adult rule at all times so that no adult is ever alone with one youth.
5. Adult volunteers with youth shall attend regular training and educational events provided by the church to keep volunteers informed of church policies and state laws regarding child abuse.
6. Adult volunteers shall immediately report to their supervisor any behavior that seems abusive or inappropriate.

Please answer each of the following questions:

1. As a volunteer in this congregation, do you agree to observe and abide by all church policies regarding working in ministries with youth?   ☐ Yes   ☐ No
2. As a volunteer in this congregation, do you agree to observe the two-adult rule at all times? ☐ Yes   ☐ No
3. As a volunteer in this congregation, do you agree to abide by the six-month rule before beginning a volunteer assignment?   ☐ Yes   ☐ No
4. As a volunteer in this congregation, do you agree to participate in training and education events provided by the church related to your volunteer assignment?   ☐ Yes   ☐ No
5. As a volunteer in this congregation, do you agree to promptly report abusive or inappropriate behavior to your supervisor?   ☐ Yes   ☐ No
6. As a volunteer in this congregation, do you agree to discuss with a minister of this congregation your experience, if any, as a survivor of child abuse?   ☐ Yes   ☐ No
   (Answering yes to this question does not automatically disqualify you from volunteering with children or youth.)
7. As a volunteer in this congregation, do you agree to inform a minister of this congregation if you have ever been convicted of child abuse?   ☐ Yes   ☐ No

I have read this **Participation Covenant**, and I agree to observe and abide by the policies set forth above.

_____

Signature of Applicant   Date

_____

Print Full Name

This is a sample form. Please tailor it to fit your congregation's specific needs.

© 2003 Discipleship Resources.

REPORT OF SUSPECTED INCIDENT OF YOUTH ABUSE

1. Name of worker (paid or volunteer) observing or receiving disclosure of abuse of youth:

   _____

2. Victim's name: _____

   Victim's age/date of birth: _____

3. Date/place of initial conversation with/report from victim: _____

   _____

4. Victim's statement (give a detailed summary here): _____

   _____

   _____

   _____

   _____

5. Name of person accused of abuse: _____

   Relationship of accused to victim (paid staff, volunteer, family member, other): _____

   _____

6. Reported to pastor: _____

   Date/time: _____

   Summary: _____

   _____

   _____

   _____

7. Call to victim's parent/guardian: _____

   Date/time: _____

   Spoke with: _____

   Summary: _____

   _____

   _____

8. Call to local children and family service agency: _____

   Date/time: _____

   Spoke with: _____

   Summary: _____

   _____

   _____

9. Call to local law enforcement agency: _____

   Date/time: _____

   Spoke with: _____

   Summary: _____

   _____

   _____

10. Other contacts: _____

   Name: _____

   Date/time: _____

   Summary: _____

   _____

   _____

   _____
   Signature of Person Making the Report   Date

This is a sample form. Please tailor your congregation's form to comply with the reporting requirements of the laws of your state and your congregation's policies.

It is imperative that the person filling out this report be familiar with the state law reporting requirements before taking any action or completing this report.

ACCIDENT REPORT FORM

(Please print all information.)

Date of accident: _____ Time of accident: _____

Name of youth injured: _____ Age: _____

Address of youth: _____

_____

Location of accident: _____

Parent or guardian: _____

Name of person (or people) who witnessed the accident:

Name: _____ Phone: _____

Name: _____ Phone: _____

Name: _____ Phone: _____

Describe accident:

_____

_____

_____

_____

_____

_____

_____

_____   _____
Signature of Person Making the Report   Date

This is a sample form. Please tailor it to fit your congregation's specific needs.

LOCAL CHURCH SELF-EVALUATION FORM

Use the following list to help your congregation assess its policy needs for the prevention of abuse in your church's youth ministry. Read each statement; then mark the appropriate response in the column to the right. By completing the form, you will be able to see at a glance the areas needing attention.

Statement	Yes	No	Unsure
1. We screen and check references for all paid employees, including clergy, who have significant contact with youth.	☐	☐	☐
2. We screen all volunteer workers for any position involving work with youth.	☐	☐	☐
3. We train at least annually all volunteer or paid workers with youth to understand the nature of abuse of youth and to recognize indicators of abuse.	☐	☐	☐
4. We train at least annually all volunteer or paid workers with youth in how to carry out our policies to prevent child abuse.	☐	☐	☐
5. Our workers are informed of state law requirements regarding abuse and their responsibility for reporting incidents.	☐	☐	☐
6. We have a clear reporting procedure for a suspected incident of abuse that follows the requirements of our state law.	☐	☐	☐
7. We have insurance coverage available in case a complaint of abuse of youth occurs.	☐	☐	☐
8. We have a clearly defined building usage strategy as a component of our abuse prevention plan.	☐	☐	☐
9. We have a clearly defined response plan to be implemented in case an allegation of abuse of youth is made against someone in our church.	☐	☐	☐
10. We offer at least annual educational opportunities to youth and parents about how to recognize and reduce risks of abuse.	☐	☐	☐
11. We take our policies to prevent abuse of youth seriously, and we are committed to their enforcement for the safety and security of all our youth.	☐	☐	☐

YOUTH MINISTRY STAFF WORKER POSITION DESCRIPTION

Position: Staff worker in the church's youth ministry programs
Reports to: Youth Director/Youth Minister/Senior Pastor

General Qualifications Required

1. All youth staff members shall be of good character and be of the Christian faith.
2. All youth staff members shall
   a. be physically, mentally, and emotionally healthy.
   b. have a basic understanding of youth and their needs.
   c. be adaptive to a variety of situations.
   d. be willing to grow in their knowledge of youth through periodic education and training events.
3. All youth staff members shall have a physician's report stating that the staff member is in good health and has presented the result of a current tuberculin test.
4. All youth staff members shall have completed the equivalent of a high school diploma.
5. All youth staff members shall be at least twenty-two years of age.

Duties of Youth Staff Member

1. Provide physical, emotional, and intellectual support to youth, as appropriate for the circumstances.
2. Provide appropriate guidance to each youth in your ministries and activities.
3. Develop a relationship of trust and continuity with the youth and their parents.
4. Provide support and assistance to parents of youth through positive communication.
5. Provide opportunities for spiritual growth through appropriate programs and worship experiences.
6. Provide opportunities for growth in knowledge and understanding of the Christian faith through appropriate programs and educational experiences with youth.
7. Create and support a youth council comprised of youth and adults to assist with implementation of youth ministry opportunities for study, worship, fellowship, and mission.
8. Coordinate weekly community-building activities, programs, and Bible study opportunities for youth.
9. Coordinate monthly mission opportunities.
10. Coordinate participation in district and conference youth activities.

Performance Expectations of a Youth Staff Member

1. Be punctual. Notify the youth director in advance if you must be late.
2. Be reliable in your attendance. Notify the youth director in advance if you must be absent.
3. Attend periodic training and education events provided by the church.
4. Be polite, friendly, and courteous to others, both youth and adults.
5. Do not engage in physical punishment/discipline of any youth.
6. Cooperate with other youth staff members, volunteers, and parents.
7. Abide by and apply the youth ministry policies of _____ Church at all times.

I have read and understand the position description for youth staff members of _____
Church. My signature indicates my agreement and covenant to abide by the requirements set forth.

_____
Signature of Applicant   Date

This is a sample form. Please adapt it to the specific needs of your congregation.

DIRECTOR OF YOUTH MINISTRY/MINISTER FOR YOUTH
POSITION DESCRIPTION

The director of youth ministry/minister for youth serves under the supervision of the senior pastor and the staff-parish relations committee and reports to the church council regularly. The director or minister for youth shall work collegially with other program and ministry staff members.

The director of youth ministry/minister for youth will advocate and model United Methodist theology, doctrine, and polity. The director of youth ministry/minister for youth will participate in district and conference connectional meetings and events, giving leadership in these settings as opportunities arise.

The director of youth ministry/minister for youth shall be at least twenty-two years old. The director/ minister for youth shall have, at a minimum, earned a high school diploma.

Responsibilities of the Director of Youth Ministry/Minister for Youth

Youth and Parents (family ministry)
- develop healthy relationships with youth and their families;
- guide youth and their families in spiritual formation and growth;
- provide support groups and/or short-term study groups for parents;
- assist in the integration of youth into the life of the whole congregation: worship, choirs, committees, missions, and so forth;
- reach out to inactive youth.

Leadership
- support, educate, and train all volunteers according to the church's and the annual conference's policies for the prevention of child abuse;
- coordinate monthly meetings of the youth council to be led by youth for the purpose of planning, implementing, and leading youth ministry in study, worship, fellowship, and mission;
- train and support a team of adult workers with youth to help supervise, guide, mentor, and lead the youth;
- coordinate parent meetings four to six times a year;
- attend continuing education events at least annually for training and spiritual growth.

Programming
- coordinate with the church council and other church committees;
- coordinate weekly UMYF programs for junior and senior highs;
- coordinate weekly Bible study, Sunday school, and DISCIPLE Bible study for junior and senior highs;
- coordinate monthly mission opportunities;
- include youth in worship leadership for the congregation as well as for the youth group;
- coordinate summer plans (missions, retreats, camps, fun, and so forth);
- coordinate participation in district, conference, jurisdictional, and General Conference activities.

Other duties as they arise in youth ministry

Responsibilities of the Church for the Director of Youth Ministry/Minister for Youth
(Fulfilling these responsibilities will help to assure the success and health of the director/minister for youth by providing benefits, education, and boundaries.)

- competitive salary;
- health insurance coverage;
- pension plan;
- continuing education funds;
- travel expense reimbursement;
- compensation time for overtime worked and for trips taken;
- vacation—at least two weeks, preferably three, per year;
- holidays as days off—same as the other church staff members.

A CELEBRATION OF OUR COMMITMENT TO YOUTH

Prelude

"They'll Know We Are Christians by Our Love" (*The Faith We Sing*, 2223), or a selection by the youth praise band.

Call to Worship

Leader: O God, by our presence here today,
People: We welcome the youth!
Leader: O God, by our promises in holy baptism and confirmation,
People: We claim the youth!
Leader: O God, by our participation in the ministries of this congregation,
People: We support the youth!
Leader: O God, by our commitment to keeping this place holy and safe in every way,
People: We surround the youth with steadfast love!
Leader: O God, in this time of worship, fill our hearts with joy as
People: We establish the youth in faith!
Leader: O God, give us wisdom, strength, and courage enough to show the world that
ALL: We celebrate the youth! Amen!

Hymn of Praise

"Sanctuary" (*The Faith We Sing*, 2164)
or "Shine, Jesus, Shine" (*The Faith We Sing*, 2173)

Congregational Prayer

Gracious and merciful God, you have brought us together in this community of faith as witnesses to your love for all youth, those here and those to come. We ask for guidance and courage as we seek to make this church a scared space for all people who come to us, especially our youth. Give us the courage to create within our ministries safe and holy places where our youth may grow in faith and in their awareness of your presence in their lives. This we ask in your Son's most holy name. Amen.

Pastoral Concerns
Silent Prayer
Pastoral Prayer
The Lord's Prayer

Old Testament Lesson

Jeremiah 1:4-19 (Have a senior-high boy read this passage. Or, as a powerful and different way to proclaim the Word, let a junior-high boy read as Jeremiah and an older adult read the narrator voice and the Lord's voice.)

Congregational Singing or Youth Choir

"Many Gifts, One Spirit" (*The United Methodist Hymnal*, 114)
"Praise to the Lord, the Almighty" (*The United Methodist Hymnal*, 139)

Gospel Lesson
Luke 2:21-24 and 40-52 (Have the Gospel read by a senior-high girl or boy, possibly in unison.)

Response to the Gospel
"Heleluyan" (*The United Methodist Hymnal*, 78)

Epistle Lesson
1 Corinthians 13 (Have a UMYF counselor or a parent from your congregation read this lesson.)

Affirmation of Faith
(*The United Methodist Hymnal*, 887)

Recognition of Youth and the Adults Who Work With Youth (Both Sunday School and Counselors)
Invite all youth and the adults who work with youth to stand. Express gratitude for those youth present and appreciation to those adults standing for their commitment to the youth ministry of your church. Applause would be an appropriate expression to those standing.

Offertory Anthem (by the congregation or youth choir)
"Psalm 139" (a musical version rather than the Psalter)
"Morning Has Broken" (*The United Methodist Hymnal*, 145)

Doxology
(*The United Methodist Hymnal*, 95)

Sermon
"Don't We All Want to Live in Sacred Space?: We Value Everyone Here—Children, Youth, and Adults"

Invitation to Christian Discipleship

Hymn of Dedication
"Lord, Be Glorified" (*The Faith We Sing*, 2150)

Benediction

Response Hymn
"Go Now in Peace" (*The United Methodist Hymnal*, 665)

Other Sources and Resources

These organizations have helpful information and resource materials about child abuse. Materials from these organizations are available on request.

Organizations

- **Childhelp USA**
  15757 N. 78th Street
  Scottsdale, AZ 85260
  www.childhelpusa.org
- **Children's Defense Fund**
  25 E Street NW
  Washington, DC 20001
  www.childrensdefense.org
- **Christian Ministry Resources**
  617 Greenbrook Pkwy
  Matthews, NC 28104
  www.churchlawtoday.com
- **FaithTrust Institute**
  2400 North 45th Street, #10
  Seattle, WA 98103
  www.faithtrustinstitute.org
- **General Commission on the Status and Role of Women**
  1200 Davis Street
  Evanston, IL 60201
  www.gcsrw.org
- **National Center for Missing and Exploited Children**
  699 Prince Street
  Alexandria, VA 22314
  www.missingkids.com
- **National Center for Prosecution of Child Abuse**
  99 Canal Center Plaza, Suite 510
  Alexandria, VA 22314
  www.ndaa-apri.org
- **National Children's Advocacy Center**
  210 Pratt Avenue
  Huntsville, AL 35801
  www.nationalcac.org
- **National Clearinghouse on Child Abuse and Neglect Information**
  330 C Street, SW
  Washington, DC 20447
  http://nccanch.acf.hhs.gov

- **National Court-Appointed Special Advocate Association**
  100 West Harrison Street
  North Tower, Suite 500
  Seattle, WA 98119
  www.casanet.org
- **Nonprofit Risk Management Center**
  1130 Seventeenth Street, NW, Suite 210
  Washington, DC 20036
  www.nonprofitrisk.org
- **Office of Children's Ministries General Board of Discipleship**
  PO Box 340003
  Nashville, TN 37203-0003
  615-340-7143
  www.gbod.org/children
- **Office of Ministries With Women, Children, and Families General Board of Global Ministries**
  475 Riverside Dr., Room 1549
  New York, NY 10115
  http://gbgm-umc.org/mission_programs/cim
- **Parents Anonymous, Inc.**
  675 West Foothill Blvd., Suite 220
  Claremont, CA 91711-3475
  www.parentsanonymous.org
- **Prevent Child Abuse America**
  200 South Michigan Avenue, 17th Floor
  Chicago, IL 60604-2404
  www.preventchildabuse.org
- **Risk Management Department General Council on Finance and Administration**
  1200 Davis Street
  Evanston, IL 60201
  www.gcfa.org/RiskManagementPage.htm
- **Your state and/or county child and family protective services department.**

Sources

These resources will guide you to many other helpful resources related to child abuse.

Resources published by Discipleship Resources may be ordered online at www.discipleshipresources.org; by phone at 800-972-0433; by fax at 615-340-7590; or by mail from Customer Services, PO Box 340012, Nashville, TN 37203-0012.

- *Behavioral Covenants in Congregations: A Handbook for Honoring Differences,* by Gilbert R. Rendle (Alban Institute, 1999).
- *The Book of Discipline of The United Methodist Church—2004* (The United Methodist Publishing House, 2004).
- *The Buck Stops Here: Legal and Ethical Responsibilities for United Methodist Organizations,* by Mary Logan (Discipleship Resources, 2000).
- *Counseling Troubled Teens and Their Families: A Handbook for Pastors and Youth Workers,* by Andrew J. Weaver, John D. Preston, and Leigh W. Jerome (Abingdon Press, 1999).
- *The Hidden Shame of the Church: Sexual Abuse of Children and the Church,* by Ron O'Grady, Risk Book Series (WCC Publications, 2001).
- *Is Nothing Sacred? The Story of a Pastor, the Women He Sexually Abused, and the Congregation He Nearly Destroyed,* by Marie M. Fortune (United Church Press, 1989).
- *Keeping the Faith: Guidance for Christian Women Facing Abuse,* by Marie M. Fortune (HarperSanFrancisco, 1995).
- *Living the Sacred Trust: A Resource on Clergy Misconduct of a Sexual Nature for Cabinets and Boards of Ordained Ministry of The United Methodist Church* (General Board of Higher Education and Ministry, 1999). Available from Cokesbury, 800-672-1789.
- *Love Does No Harm: Sexual Ethics for the Rest of Us,* by Marie M. Fortune (Continuum Publishing Group, 1995).
- *Mission Accomplished: A Practical Guide to Risk Management for Nonprofits,* second edition, by Peggy M. Jackson, Leslie T. White, and Melanie L. Herman (Nonprofit Risk Management Center, 1999).
- *Not If, But When* (United Methodist Communications, 1999). Item # 11-45-5. Phone: 888-346-3862.
- *Preventing Child Sexual Abuse: A Curriculum for Children Ages Nine Through Twelve,* by Kathryn Goering Reid and Marie M. Fortune (United Church Press, 1989).
- *Reaching for the Light: A Guide for Ritual Abuse Survivors and Their Therapists,* by Emilie P. Rose (Pilgrim Press, 1996).
- *Safe and Secure: The Alban Guide to Protecting Your Congregation,* by Jeffrey W. Hanna (Alban Institute, 1999).
- *Sexual Abuse Prevention: A Course of Study for Teenagers,* revised edition, by Rebecca Voelkel-Haugen and Marie M. Fortune (Pilgrim Press, 1996).
- *Staff Screening Tool Kit: Building a Strong Foundation Through Careful Staffing,* third edition, by John C. Patterson (Nonprofit Risk Management Center, 2004).
- *Staying Safe at School: What You Need to Know,* by Chester Quarles (Broadman & Holman Publishers, 2000).
- *Survivor Prayers: Talking With God About Childhood Sexual Abuse,* by Catherine J. Foote (Westminster John Knox Press, 1994).
- *Taking the High Road: A Guide to Effective and Legal Employment Practices for Nonprofits,* by Jennifer C. Hauge and Melanie L. Herman (Nonprofit Risk Management Center, 1999).
- *United Methodist Youth Handbook,* by Micheal Selleck (Discipleship Resources, 1999).
- *Violence in the Family: A Workshop Curriculum for Clergy and Other Helpers,* by Marie M. Fortune (Pilgrim Press, 1991).
- *Welcome the Child: A Child Advocacy Guide for Churches,* by Shannon P. Daley and Kathleen A. Guy (Friendship Press, 1994).

Videos

- *Bless Our Children: Preventing Sexual Abuse* (40 minutes). Story of one congregation's efforts to provide abuse prevention information for their children. Available from FaithTrust Institute, 877-860-2255.
- *Caring Shepherds* (18 minutes). Created to help congregational leaders identify potential problems and develop policies to reduce the occurrence of sexual abuse and misconduct. Available from the Risk Management Department of the General Council on Finance and Administration of The United Methodist Church, 847-425-6560.
- *Hear Their Cries: Religious Responses to Child Abuse* (48 minutes). Provides definitions related to abuse, signs for recognizing abuse, and examples of how to respond. Available from FaithTrust Institute, 877-860-2255.
- *Safe Sanctuaries for Children and Youth: Reducing the Risk of Abuse in the Church* (90 minutes; VHS or DVD). Provides additional support for assessing the risk of abuse and implementing processes to reduce that risk; designed for use with *Safe Sanctuaries* and *Safe Sanctuaries for Youth.* Available from Discipleship Resources (see ordering information at the top of this page).